learning to
trust
again

Dedication:

For my parents, who traveled this journey with me
and felt each bump in the road.
It is because you loved me, believed me,
and taught me about Jesus
that I'm where I am today.

Discovery House Publishers

Books, music, and videos that feed the soul with the Word of God

Box 3566 Grand Rapids, MI 49501

learning to
trust
again

a young woman's journey

of healing from sexual abuse

christa sands
edited by joyce k. ellis

Learning to Trust Again
Copyright © 1999 by Christa Sands

Discovery House Publishers is affiliated with RBC Ministries, Grand Rapids, Michigan 49512.

Library of Congress Cataloging-in-Publication Data

Sands, Christa J.
    Learning to trust again : a young woman's journey of healing from sexual abuse / by Christa Sands : edited by Joyce K. Ellis.
        p.   cm.
    ISBN 1-57293-055-1
    1. Child sexual abuse—United States Case studies. 2. Sexually abused children—United States Case studies. 3. Girls—Crimes against—United States Case studies. 4. Sands, Christa, 1976– 5. Adult child sexual abuse victims—United States Biography. 6. Adult child sexual abuse victims—Religious life—United States. I. Ellis, Joyce K. II. Title.
    HV6570.7.S35   1999
    362.76'4'092—dc21   99-41523
    [B]   CIP

Printed in the United States of America
99 00 01 02 03 04 05
/ CHG /
1 3 5 7 9 10 8 6 4 2

Contents

Foreword

In my twenty-five years of counseling sexual abuse victims and offenders, I've worked with hundreds of women like Christa Sands who were sexually abused as children. There is nothing more powerful than the personal story of a first-hand experience with the devastation and destruction of sexual abuse.

As Christa's story well illustrates, the abusers' shameful acts and lies steal the victims' innocence and self-identity and distort these precious children's view of God. If the victims pray for the abuse to stop, and it doesn't, they may think that God doesn't care, that they don't deserve to be helped, or that God is punishing them for the abuse. These lies will follow the children into adulthood and greatly hinder their ability to trust God, believe His Word, or fully participate in fellowship with believers in the local church.

With this book Christa celebrates her "freedom day," the day she told her parents she had been sexually abused. It was a day of courage, truth, and the beginning of her pilgrimage toward freedom. Christa is like many other victims whose shame and fear hold them in bondage for years. But in one respect, Christa's story is unusual because she told her secret and began her healing process during adolescence. Most adolescents don't want to deal with it. They say, "Let's forget about it. I want to get on with my life." Consequently, they bury all their hurt and shame for twenty, thirty, or forty years—even a lifetime. Sometimes it can't be hidden any longer and creates much greater problems in adulthood. Or they develop dependencies on alcohol, drugs, food, or prescription medications to dull their pain.

During these years of silence their shame-filled identity, their difficulty in developing intimate relationships based on trust, and their distorted view of God may lead them to make poor decisions in relationships and other areas of life.

In my research project for a Ph.D. in counseling psychology, victims reported shame as the most damaging symptom of sexual abuse. Seeing themselves as "bad" or "defective" people, they feel they don't measure up to their own standards or the standards of others. They try to prove to God or others that they are important or special (i.e., by overachievement, by needing to be right, by being the best at everything). They may even punish themselves physically (e.g., cutting themselves, burning themselves with cigarettes). They may punish themselves emotionally by setting themselves up to be hurt or rejected by others, or shaming themselves through negative or destructive self-talk.

Although Christa didn't exhibit some of the more severe examples of physical self-punishment, she did develop classic defense mechanisms to survive the abuse and keep the secret. She shares that "deep roots of shame began to choke my soul. I retreated to my inner world and wore a mask to cope with the outer world." She rationalized the crime, minimizing the perpetrator's act in her own mind, and withdrawing from others because of her feelings of shame and insecurity. She suppressed the bad memories so they wouldn't interfere with her life, and used the defense mechanism of "splitting" (by pretending to be asleep, entering a fantasy world, and daydreaming) to deal with the pain of the abuse.

As child victims become adolescents and mature into adulthood, these defense mechanisms interfere with their ability to feel and express their emotions, deal with relationships, function in everyday life in a healthy manner, and understand why they feel and behave as they do.

> **When we pressure victims to let go of the anger quickly and forgive the perpetrator, we don't realize that premature forgiveness can actually hinder the healing process.**

Often the Christian community doesn't know how to deal with these issues. Some people in the church don't understand that anger is a natural response to being sexually abused and a defense against being hurt again. When we pressure victims to let go of the anger quickly and forgive the perpetrator, we don't realize that premature forgiveness can actually hinder the healing process.

Christa's experience with journaling and writing a letter to her abuser shows how a person can work through many of these difficult issues over time and come to a point of forgiveness when spiritually and emotionally strong enough to do so.

I believe the most important element in the healing process is for victims to hear and internalize truth from God's Word and to receive love, prayer, and support from God's people during this long healing journey.

I admire Christa's courage, candidness, and passion that resulted in this book. It clearly shows what God has done in her life, the importance of His Word in the healing process, and how He can redeem a very difficult life experience to help others. The Scripture references at the end of some of the chapters can be a helpful resource to help victims renew their mind with Truth.

Learning to Trust Again can help pastors, Christian counselors, victims, their families, friends, and other people in the church to empathize and understand the deep pain and emotional upheaval caused by abuse. It can also give courage to other victims who may still be afraid to share their secret and seek the help they need.

Because abuse brings extreme trauma to an entire family, family members often become almost paralyzed with fear and anger and don't know how to handle the situation. Christa's book is an excellent resource for parents and other helpers, offering clear, step-by-step guidelines regarding how to respond when a child tells them about abuse, how to report this crime to authorities, and how to support the child and get help for themselves after they find out about the abuse.

It's a sad reality that sexual abuse happens—even in the church community. Satan has done his evil work, but there is still hope. Christ the Healer, can bring truth, light, and healing out of the dark ashes of the abuse.

Jeanette Vought, Ph.D.

coauthor with Lynn Heitritter, *Helping Victims of Sexual Abuse* licensed psychologist (L.P.) and marriage and family therapist, certified criminal justice specialist, and Founder and executive director of the Christian Recovery Center, Minneapolis, Minnesota

Acknowledgments

I'm thankful for the opportunity to thank a few of the many individuals who supported me in my healing process and the writing of this book, including:

Cherry Davis for compassion when I needed it most and help in getting my story in the newspaper. Sharon Van Kley for letting me cry and vent, and for caring enough to go to bat for me amongst the "powers that be" at BEA so that I could make a difference. Craig Van Kley for volunteering me to speak. Thanks for being a support by sharing the podium with me!

The 1992–1993 BEA Project TRUST troop for caring about me. Tawnya Ristau for your friendship that helped me through. Eric Thomas for gently pushing me to take risks. Your encouragement, advice, and support has done much to help me grow and heal. Sharon Hoyt for going the extra mile in extending compassion to a hurting soul. You endured my many interruptions, welcomed me into your office, and helped me see myself as a person of worth. You were key in my healing process.

Don Helmstetter for your example of compassion. Those at Community Covenant Church who prayed for me. My Northwestern College friends who believed in me from the start, encouraged me when I felt overwhelmed or defeated, and faithfully prayed this book into being: Jody Renner, Sarah Severson, Michelle Sasse, Heidi Kuehnast, Candace Hauge, Andrea Nybo, Melinda Eisenlohr, and Jill McCune.

Everyone at Discovery House Publishers for believing in a young, unknown writer. I am grateful to be working with people who view publishing as a ministry more than a business.

Joyce Ellis for your expertise as editor. I prayed for an editor who would understand my newness to the world of publishing as well as the difficulty I'd face in seeing my "baby" changed. God answered my prayer! Thank you for your patience with me, your willingness to explain procedures, and your flexibility in working via e-mail once I moved to California. Thanks, especially, for your prayers for and belief in this book.

All my extended family for caring about me and praying me through this process. Grandma Larry and Morrie for your unwavering belief that this book would be published. Thank you for your constant love and support. Grandma Esther and Grandpa Jerry for faithfully up lifting my book and me in prayer. Thank you for being godly examples to us grandkids. Kyle for getting off the computer every time I needed it and for keeping me humble! I couldn't ask for a better brother.

My parents, Gary and Carol, for your 100-percent support of every new dream or experience I want to pursue. Your prayers, pep talks, and advice kept me focused on what I believed God was calling me to do. Your generosity in relieving my financial concerns and allowing me to use (monopolize) the computer and take the car back and forth from school every weekend enabled me to make this dream of mine come true. Thanks for believing in me when I didn't believe in myself.

My Co-Writer, Jesus Christ, for I would not have a story to write had You not lifted me out of the pit and given me a firm place to stand (Psalm 40:2). Nor would I have made it through the first month of writing, let alone the last two years had You not provided me with the discipline, determination, and passion to see this project through. You have taught me much about faith as You've taken my inexperience and turned me into an author. Truly anything is possible with You!

A Note to My Readers

March 17, 1997

While others are celebrating St. Patrick's Day, I am celebrating what I call my Freedom Day. Six years ago today I mustered all the courage inside me and told my parents I had been sexually abused. After living for eight years with this poisonous secret, it was a relief to purge its venom and finally seek help. This day is a day of remembrance for me. A day to look back with joy and thanksgiving as I see the path of healing on which God has walked with me. A day to reflect on all the changes I have undergone. A day to ponder the changes still needed and the paths God may lead me on in the future. A day of hope. A day of peace.

But this year, March 17 has special meaning to me as I venture into the unknown and, at times, overwhelming territory of writing a book. Six years ago, when I started journaling about issues I was facing, I dreamed of writing my story to give hope to others who have been sexually abused, helping them see that they, too, can make it through. Yet God, in His perfect wisdom, told me "not yet" and put my dream on hold. My own healing process had barely begun, and I had only touched the surface of many issues I had to bring to God's healing light.

So my journal became a therapeutic outlet during the healing process. Though I struggled with doubts, fearing my dream of writing a book was too big, I began praying that if this desire was not from God that He would replace it with another dream. But it never went away. In fact, the further I went in my healing process, the stronger the desire to write became.

I think it's only fitting that I begin what I call my "faith project" on the anniversary of when my dream began. God has a neat way of working things out, doesn't He?

So here I am on the brink of the unknown. Excitement mixes with doubt. A little voice inside my head still taunts me: *Will I be able to pull this off? What do I know about writing a book?* Yet I am reminded of some encouragement I received from one of my professors. I told him, "People my age don't write books!" And he said, "No, people with passion write books." I know he's right, for it is my passion for making a difference and helping people that drives me.

I'm moving ahead by faith, knowing that nothing—even my big dream—is too big for God (Matthew 19:26). And so I place my dream in His hands and wait in eager anticipation to see where He leads me.

As you read this book, you will find some insights I have gained as I've looked back and sorted through the memories of this journey. I didn't always see these things at the time, but as I've studied Scripture, done some reading in the area of sexual abuse, and grown in my own healing process, the Lord has given me better perspective.

We have also changed some names and details to protect those who do not need to be hurt further in the telling of my story.

My prayer for six years has been that God would use me and my pain for His glory. He heard my prayer. It just took Him six years to answer! And so, this, my Freedom Day, reminds me of God's faithfulness. No matter what lies ahead, I have nothing to fear. He has given me the hope, the passion, and the green light. All I have to do is provide the details.

Christa Sands

Introduction

*You will know the truth,
and the truth will set you free.*

John 8:32

Ignorance is bliss . . . but it is "killing" society's most precious resource—its children. Satan uses our ignorance for his gain as he chokes the innocence out of millions of children wounded by abuse. Fear, the root of our ignorance, is Satan's weapon to silence us and make us believe that if we don't talk about the evil it will go away.

- Out of fear a teacher who sees signs of abuse avoids getting involved.

- Out of fear a minister denies that one of his members could do such a thing to a child.

- Out of fear a parent refuses to put two and two together and name the evil.

- Out of fear victims live in terror that someone may find out their secret, and they somehow blame themselves for what happened.

- Out of fear all of us find the dark of silence safer than the light of truth.

Yet Satan's weapon of fear is not nearly as powerful as the resulting silence that imprisons us. In our ignorance we protect the guilty and leave the innocent shouting inaudible cries for mercy.

Some definitions

According to the National Committee to Prevent Child Abuse, child sexual abuse is sexual contact between a child and adult or older child for the sexual gratification of the offender. It includes physical contact, such as handling of the child's or the offender's genitals or breasts, oral sex, or attempted or actual penetration of the child's vagina or rectum; and nonphysical contact, such as forcing a child to look at the offender's genitals, exposure of a child's genitals, talking to a child in a sexually explicit manner, peeping at a child in the bath or while he or she is undressing (voyeurism), exposing a child to pornographic materials, or exploiting a child through pornography or prostitution.

Epidemic proportions

Many people ignore the issue of sexual abuse because they think it will never affect them personally. Statistics show otherwise: At least one in four females and one in six males is sexually abused by the age of eighteen. Youth expert Dawson McAllister reports that 25 percent of the nation's 20 million teenagers have been sexually abused.

One senior law enforcement official said, "The only way not to find the problem in your community is simply not to look."[1]

Perry Draper, an abuse survivor and family therapist,

agrees. "If sexual abuse were a biological disease, it would be declared a major epidemic of catastrophic proportions," he writes. "The whole country would be mobilized toward treatment and prevention of any further outbreak."[2]

Victims span all ages from infants to age eighteen. (In this book I use the general term *children* to refer to victims of abuse—not to ignore the high number of teenagers who are abused, but as an inclusive term, covering both younger and older victims.) The FBI reports that most rape victims are between ages ten and nineteen, while a quarter of them are younger than age twelve.[3]

Although sexual abuse is shockingly prevalent, cultural taboos keep victims in silence and potential helpers in ignorance. Research shows that a child is molested every two-and-a-half minutes, yet only a fraction of these crimes—less than 10 percent—are reported. For every victim known, at least nine remain hidden.[4]

Conspiracy of silence

Most victims are too ashamed to speak out. This is especially true for males. Society gives them confusing messages:

    a. They should be pleased with any kind of sexual experience.

    b. If they were tough enough or masculine enough, something like this wouldn't happen.

If the abuser was a male, male victims often fear being labeled homosexual. No wonder many hide in silence—no matter what the cost—rather than exposing the truth.

An article in *Glamour* magazine reports:

"In a recent study of eight hundred college students who were sexually abused as children, 63 percent of the women and 73 percent of the men had never told anyone about the experience . . . . Some . . . may be able to mask their anxieties for years, creating what experts call 'a psychological time bomb.' Guilt, confusion, depression and passivity can suddenly explode into . . . self-destructive behavior . . . even suicide. Long-term symptoms include detachment from others and frightening flashbacks."[5]

Sexual abuse is one of the root causes of many of today's social problems. When society deals only with the effects of the abuse, and "pulls the weed," the root continues to fester and grow. Satan's subtle strategy keeps society and innocent victims in denial, for he knows that until victims deal with the root of the problem, their lives will never be full and complete.

There is no typical victim. There is no typical abuser. Abuse crosses all racial, religious, and socioeconomic lines. The victims are our relatives, friends, and neighbors. Sadly, the perpetrators are also our relatives, friends, and neighbors. It is a myth that children are most likely to be sexually abused by a stranger. In at least 85 percent of the cases, the child knows—and may even be related to—the offender.[6]

A battle rages: lies vs. truth

Fear and ignorance stop many from getting involved, leaving children to fight the difficult battle for survival themselves. No one would think of sending children off to war to fight for freedom, yet we hesitate to join victims of sexual abuse at the front lines in their own battle for freedom. May we never forget that the worst thing in a war is to be in the heat of battle without reinforcements.

Some people will never know the terrible secret that victims must deal with.

But I know. I am a victim of sexual abuse. For eight years I lived in festering silence, trying to survive. From the trenches of a battle no less devastating than any global conflict, I bring a message for other victims of this war for healing:

1. We must break the silence.

2. We must help others understand the prevalence and devastation of sexual abuse.

3. We must find hope in the fact that healing and wholeness are not only possible but worth the journey through pain.

Satan is out to demolish God's kingdom. What better way than to harm children at such an influential age that the wounds they suffer can block them from experiencing God's love and healing growth for the rest of their lives?

His weapon of abuse spreads lies children easily believe because they do not have the maturity to understand their experiences, lies such as these:

- *The abuse was your fault.* Satan covers us with such deep shame that we blame ourselves for the abuse and develop a deep loathing of ourselves. How can we think that God could love or want to use anyone like us?

- *No one can be trusted.* Satan wins the battle if he can shatter children's trust in God, other people, and themselves. Trust is precious, and once it is gone, it's not easily relearned. Children who can't trust don't believe they are worthy of God's love or anyone else's. They grow up to become adults who believe the same lies Satan whispered in their ears long before. The abuse becomes a wall between the victim and a God who seemed unable or unwilling to stop the horrific nightmare. How can we allow God, whom we don't trust, to fill us with His love, to heal us, and use us?

- *If you forget about the trauma, the pain will disappear.* Though we become numb to the pain, the wounds we suffered in childhood become deeply infected under the surface. We want to believe Satan's lie, but instead the pain festers inside, causing increasing damage to our already wounded souls.

- *If you tell people about your abuse, they will think you are bad.* Satan, the Prince of Darkness, wants us to remain in our silent pits of darkness and shame. Silent victims suffer alone, devoid of the healing power of community, of relationships with God and others. Satan presses us to hide, and we comply, believing his lie that exposure would destroy us.

Our powerful offensive weapon

The dark power of abuse cannot survive in the light. "Everyone who does evil hates the light, and will not come into the light for fear that his deeds will be exposed" (John 3:20). Satan is the concealer, but God is the revealer. "He reveals the deep things of darkness and brings deep shadows into the light" (Job 12:22).

In Ephesians 5:11, God commands us to "have nothing to do with the fruitless deeds of darkness, but rather expose them." Verse 12 may seem to contradict verse eleven, but God is saying He knows about the shame that enfolds us when we risk audibly speaking about the acts of darkness and betrayal that the abuser has done to us: "For it is shameful even to mention what the disobedient do in secret" (v. 11).

[1]Perry L. Draper, *Haunted Memories* (Grand Rapids: Fleming H. Revell, 1996), p. 35.

[2]Dawson McAllister, "Teenagers Are Begging: 'Feel My Pain!'" *Decision* (January 1997), p. 9.

[3]Terry Casey, "Child Sexual Abuse: It Is Happening and Our Children Need Protecting," *Sexual Assault Program of Northern St. Louis County, MN* (June 1994), p. 14.

[4]Lois Timnick, "22 Percent in Survey were Child Abuse Victims," *Los Angeles Times* (August 25, 1985).

[5]Katie O'Neil, "The Chilling Facts About Sexual Abuse," *Glamour,* (June 1984), p. 265.

[6]Casey, *Sexual Assault Program of Northern St. Louis County, MN* (June 1994), p. 14.

CHAPTER 1

A Deep, Dark Pit

Terrors overwhelm me; my dignity is driven away as by the wind, my safety vanishes like a cloud.

Job 30:15

Balancing was the hardest part. Once we took the training wheels off, my life was in the hands of "Walter," our close family friend. I still remember pedaling around his driveway with his hands on the back of the seat and handle-bar. I wobbled all over the place, and at times I became so discouraged I wanted to give up, but I was determined to do it on my own. I didn't want him hanging onto me anymore. So with fierce determination, I faced the hard work and continual practice of learning to ride a "real" bike. I refused to give up. And finally the day came when I took off on my own! As the wind brushed my face, pride swelled in my heart. I had broken free!

Years later, as I reflected on that memory, I saw a dark similarity between it and the abuse I suffered from this same family friend. My abuser, Walter, maintained a powerful hold on me long after the abuse. My emotional, mental, and spiritual "equilibrium" wobbled so much that I thought I would never get straightened out. I lost hope. I wanted to give up, yet something stirred deep within me, something that made me determined not to give up and stay in bondage to this man forever.

I would need that determination because I faced a lot of "scraped knees" and "bruised elbows" along the journey toward healing—learning lessons I needed to learn, changing what I needed to change, and growing into the person God wants me to become. Slowly, my abuser's grip on my life has loosened, and I've broken free.

This is the story of my deepest heartache and my greatest victory.

Like a thief in the night

Walter and his wife were like grandparents to me and good friends of my mom and dad. I trusted Walter completely. He seemed to be a kind man, often volunteering to do favors for my family.

From these childhood years in a small Minnesota town, I have many memories of biking to their house with my brother and playing board games with them for hours around a little table in the living room. They would also read stories to us. My brother and I had fun playing outside, running around the yard, climbing trees, and exploring. Walter's wife always had cookies for us, and we ate as many as we dared! He and his wife often baby-sat for my brother and me. We would go over to their house until bedtime, then Walter drove us back home, put us to bed, and stayed until our parents came home.

I enjoyed many happy times with them, yet another emotion started pushing its way forward—an emotion I later identified as fear. Sometimes Walter wouldn't play with us. But that was okay because I was beginning to feel uncomfortable around him. By then the abuse had begun.

I was in first grade.

The recollection of the first time Walter abused me is clearly etched in my memory. (It served as a pattern for later incidents.) My parents went out for an evening alone, so Walter came over to baby-sit. After a while he tucked my brother and me into bed. The lights were out and we were supposed to go to sleep, but for some reason I lay wide awake for a long time. Then I heard his footsteps on the stairs.

As my door creaked open, I quickly shut my eyes. Apparently satisfied that I was sleeping, he walked to the bathroom and switched on the light. From my bed I dared open my eyes and could see that he had taken a tube of toothpaste out of the cabinet and was squeezing some onto his finger. I wondered what he was doing, then he turned around and started walking toward me. I quickly shut my eyes so he wouldn't see that I was awake.

With my eyes closed I began feeling and hearing the sheets and blankets being lifted up. As I lay there perfectly still, scared to swallow or even breathe, his trembling hands lifted up my underwear. He then fondled me, rubbing the toothpaste on me. After a few minutes he left me alone.

Imagine the feelings of a little first-grader! My first reaction was pure shock. I didn't understand what was happening. I was hurt and confused.

Confusion, fear, and rationalization

I remember trying to rationalize what he had just done. I thought maybe I had something wrong with my private parts and that Mom and Dad had left instructions for him to put medicine there. *Yeah, that was it!* I thought. The toothpaste was actually medicine. But if it was medicine, why did I feel so ashamed and dirty and so sure that what he had done was wrong? I lay in bed, drenched in fear and confusion.

It's amazing that I knew it was wrong because I don't remember learning about good and bad touches. I don't recall my parents ever talking to me about sexual abuse. My parents had not even told me about sex yet, so I was terrified I would get pregnant and my parents would be upset with me. In my first-grade logic, that all-consuming terror haunted me.

I was almost sure that what Walter had done was wrong, but either consciously or unconsciously I decided to do nothing about it. I remember thinking that if I told my parents and it really was medicine, then I would be embarrassed. Besides, if I told them, they probably wouldn't believe me. I was just a little girl, and he was an adult. My parents never gave me any reason to think that they wouldn't believe me, but then we had never talked about what to do in case something like that happened.

My little-girl mind reasoned that adults listen to adults, not to kids. At that age I looked to grown-ups for security and protection, fully expecting them always to do what is right. Children are taught to listen to adults and obey them. They have the power. Abuse steals the small measure of power children have, so they feel they have no choice but to remain silent. So I blamed myself and kept my mouth shut, believing that grown-ups are always right.

> Why, O Lord, do you stand far off?
>
> Why do you hide yourself
>   in times of trouble?
> In his arrogance the
>   wicked man hunts
>   down the weak,
> who are caught in the
>   schemes he devises. . . .
> He lies in wait like a lion
>   in cover;
> he lies in wait to catch the
>   helpless . . .
> He says to himself,
>   "God has forgotten;
> he covers his face and
>   never sees."
> But you, O God, do see
>   trouble and grief;
> you consider it to take it
>   in hand.
> The victim commits himself
>   to you;
> you are the helper of the
>   fatherless.
>
> PSALM 10:1–2,9,11,14

29

Years later I would learn that in that first moment of abuse he violated not only my body but also the very depths of my being. In an instant he broke the trust I had with him and with all men.

> **"I tried to wash him away,
> his crime, his smell, his violation.
> All that washed away was my innocence."**
>
> *Victim's message on a shirt for The Clothesline Project.[1]*

Stolen innocence

The next day was business as usual, at least for the rest of the world. As I went to school, I was scared that people could tell what had happened just by looking at me. Fear gripped tightly. I remember feeling as though I was watching my world go by, and I was no longer a part of it. I didn't feel normal anymore. Things like playing with dolls and climbing on the jungle gym no longer seemed important. In a matter of moments, my innocence had been stolen and my perspective on life changed forever.

I felt dirty and embarrassed, certain that if others found out what happened they would be disgusted with me. I had to hide, but where? Unconsciously I decided the only safe place for me was far down inside myself. No one could hurt me there. No one could see how awful I was. Deep roots of shame began to choke my soul. I retreated to my inner world and wore a mask to cope with the outer world.

I know the first incident of abuse happened in first grade because I remember walking from my first-grade classroom to the bathroom diagonally across the hall. I went into the stall, pulled down my pants, and bent my head as far as it would go to try to smell the toothpaste I was positive was there—to prove to myself that Walter did not put medicine on me, to prove to myself that what he had done was wrong.

As I sat in that bathroom stall, extremely confused, I wished I could tell someone. But who would believe me? I was terrified. The one thought that kept running through my head was, *Why? Why did he touch me like that?*

Forever hanging in the gallery of my mind is the portrait of that frightened little girl abruptly snatched from innocence and hurled into an evil and adult world.

Silent lamb

The abuse continued for about a year. I felt powerless to stop Walter's advances. Control over my own body was cruelly stolen from me. I don't recall exactly how many times he abused me or when it stopped, but I came to expect the abuse.

I would lie in bed fighting off sleep, determined that I wouldn't let him catch me off guard, waiting for him to get it over with. I knew exactly what he was going to do and how. I knew that when I heard his footsteps on the stairs I'd better close my eyes and lie motionless. I didn't want to get punished for being awake so late. I got so used to the abuse that I became an expert at breathing in rhythm, knowing when to swallow, and finding the right position to "sleep" in—all at age seven.

One time when my brother and I had to sleep over at Walter's house, I slept on the living room floor a few feet away from Walter's bedroom. I had no idea what to expect that night, but I was terrified, wondering if he would try anything with his wife and my brother there.

I prayed—no, pleaded—with God to keep Walter away from me. I fought sleep, yet my young body needed the rest, so I fell asleep against my will. To my knowledge Walter did not touch me that night. I don't know why God didn't keep him away other times, but I'm thankful for that one night of reprieve.

No one to trust

As a little first-grader, the abuse forced me to "grow up" quickly. Everything I thought to be true about the world exploded in my face. I learned too early that this world is more than toys, family, and learning the ABCs. I learned, instead, that the people you trust most can take the most away from you.

I felt I had nowhere to turn. I loved my parents, but I didn't want to risk their siding with Walter and confirming the "badness" I already felt deep within. I didn't have anyone else I could confide in. Walter had already proved that people weren't trustworthy.

But my secret grew so menacing I felt I had to tell someone. One time, shortly after the abuse began, I came close to telling two friends at school. In physical education class, we were playing a game, running from one end of the gym to the other. My friends were on the opposite side, and I decided to tell them when I got there. Unfortunately, by the time I reached them, fear choked me into silence. I didn't know what they would say or do or even if they would believe me.

As a first-grader, it took a lot of energy to keep silent—energy I needed for interacting with family, playing with friends, and doing schoolwork. But thinking no one could help me, I tried to protect myself, burying the painful truth deep within. That's how I survived. For eight years I lived in silence.

Important Truths About Sexual Abuse

1. Sexual abuse is a betrayal of trust. The degree of suffering does not depend solely on the specific sexual act or frequency of abuse. It takes only seconds to betray a child and forever alter his or her life.

2. The abuser often establishes a strong relationship with the child before the abuse starts.

   a. Some abusers take advantage of work or volunteer positions that offer easy access to kids: coaches, teachers, youth workers, camp counselors, and baby-sitters.

   b. Some abusers bribe children with gifts.

3. Often the abuser does not need to use force. In a relationship built on trust and dependency, the child feels as though he or she has little choice.

4. Abuse is often progressive, moving from good touch to confusing touch to outright abuse. The confusion makes the child feel like an accomplice for not stopping the abuse.

5. Abusers often try to disguise the abuse in acceptable behaviors: tickling, bathing, diapering, hugging, kissing. The child becomes confused, wondering if what he or she experienced really was abuse. Children need to trust "gut feelings." Abuse usually leaves the child feeling uncomfortable, embarrassed, or dirty.

Cautions for Parents

1. Maintain a precarious balance between trust and awareness. Abuse can happen to anyone. Someone your family knows may be a victim. Someone your family knows may be an abuser. But avoid being overly suspicious.

2. Educate your kids about personal body safety, including the following:

   a. The difference between good and bad touch. (Children need to know they have power over their own bodies.)

   b. The right to say no to whatever makes them feel uncomfortable, even if a friend or relative is abusing them. (Many parents warn kids about saying no to strangers but don't think to tell them to say no to anyone close to them if they experience bad touch.)

3. Talk to your children about sex early. Many times children have already been abused by the time their parents decide to talk to their kids about these sensitive subjects. But age-appropriate knowledge is a gift.

4. Create an open family environment so that if the children are ever in a potentially abusive situation, they feel comfortable telling you.

Reasons children don't tell

1. Fear

   a. of the abuser—Often the abuser threatens to harm the child or the child's family if the secret comes out.

   b. of not being believed—Often the child reasons that adults are older and wiser and always right, so why would parents (teachers, other adults) believe the child is telling the truth and the adult is lying? They may also fear that their parents will believe they're imagining things or making up the story.

   c. of being punished for causing the abuse.

2. Blaming themselves. *Since grown-ups are "always right,"* the child reasons, *I must have done something wrong to cause this.* The child views the abuse as punishment for being a bad person. Children may think they were abused because there is something wrong with them, that they are bad or dirty. Though many children are manipulated, bribed, or tricked into sexual abuse, victims still blame themselves. Some abusers convince victims that they enjoyed the abuse or they wouldn't have let it continue. So victims are ashamed to tell.

3. Poor self-esteem or powerlessness. When a trusted friend or loved one uses the child's little body for selfish purposes, the child often feels unworthy of safety and protection.

4. Denial. Pretending it never happened is a defense mechanism children use to try to make sense of the world and maintain their sanity.

5. Trying to keep the family together. If the abuser is a family member, silence is the price children choose to pay in order to maintain some stability and security in their chaotic world. It seems their only option.

6. Confusion. Many question whether they really were abused. They can't accept the notion that someone they trust and/or love could abuse them.

[1]The Clothesline Project is a traveling memorial to women victims of violence (such as sexual abuse, battering, and murder). To educate the public and help survivors in their healing process The Clothesline Project displays T-shirts—often with thought-provoking messages—designed by violence survivors or friends and families of women who were killed.

CHAPTER 2

A Time to Survive, A Time to Live

Why did I ever come out of the womb to see trouble and sorrow and to end my days in shame?

Jeremiah 20:18

Because the abuse happened when my opinion of myself was being formed, a deep sense of shame molded the core of my being. Shame differs from guilt in that guilt says, "What I did was bad" while shame says, "I am bad." I never had the chance to view myself as a capable human being worthy of love and respect just for being me. My abuser took away something much more valuable than any material possession. He took away my worth as a person.

> "If you could see
> the pain inside of me,
> you would die
> a thousand deaths.
> But why can't I?
> You killed my soul,
> but not my body.
> The darkness hides
> my shame.
> I fear light.
> There is safety in darkness."
>
> **Message on a shirt for
> The Clothesline Project**

I don't recall ever feeling good about myself, but by seventh grade a near-constant self-image battle raged. I hated myself. People may have noticed the fruit of low self-esteem, but the soil of shame that nurtured it remained hidden.

Insecurities magnified

The abuse magnified a hundred times the common insecurities of adolescence. I never felt good enough. I felt like a failure, useless, defective, incapable, insignificant, worthless. I thought everyone else was much more important than I ever could be. I felt like damaged goods. How could anyone ever love me?

My low self-esteem quickly became self-loathing. I believed I was repulsive and that nothing I did mattered. I think that is exactly what Satan wanted me to believe. People with deep self-hatred never take risks or take the initiative for healing, personal growth, and the fulfillment of God's will in their lives. Feeling small and useless, they won't do much for the kingdom of God.

During puberty, as I started to develop physically, I came to despise my body and tried to hide it. I'm grateful I

April 25, 1990 (age 14)

*This year has been extremely painful for me because of all the
fights with my friends. I feel people don't really like me and
that there's always someone better to be with than me. That
tears me apart. It hurts so much when I see my friends talking
and joking around with people I'd like to be friends with, too.
But I'm worried it's too late. People already have a certain
impression of me, and I can't change that. I wish I could.*

*Many people think I'm stuck-up or that I think I'm better than
everyone else. One reason I don't talk to anyone is that I'm
afraid they won't like me and they'll hurt my feelings. Another
reason is that I don't know what to say to people I don't know
very well. Contrary to popular belief, I really don't like myself.
In fact there are a million people I'd rather be. I think I'm fat,
ugly, and have no personality. People have told me I have no
personality. I guess you can't hide the truth. . . .*

didn't struggle with sexual orientation as some sexual abuse
survivors do, but when I began menstruating, I cried in bed
for days. This passage into womanhood, sometimes celebrated, made me feel dirtier than ever. Fear and revulsion
swept over me. If I could have stopped all these inevitable
physical changes, I would have. As I struggled for some feeling of worth, the weighted blanket of shame seemed impossible to lift.

Therapist E. Sue Blume describes well how I felt: "Feeling dirty becomes a part of her character rather than the response to an event that happened to her."[1]"

Extremely self-conscious and insecure about the way I looked, I compulsively checked my appearance in mirrors dozens of times a day. I panicked if I thought I lost the little hand-held mirror I always carried. It was definitely a victory when I no longer felt compelled to take it with me. Yet other signs of my internal struggle remained.

If anyone complimented me on the way I looked or something I did or said, my mind rejected it. What they said did not match what I believed about myself; so I didn't believe them.

I couldn't accept criticism, either—even if it was constructive. I became defensive, grasping for whatever shreds of hope I could find that I was a decent human being. I became overly sensitive, reading things into people's words and actions. The slightest hint of rejection cut through me like a sword and hurled me into depression for days. I became my own worst judge. Having condemned myself, I heard condemnation in other people's comments. I replayed hurtful and embarrassing situations over and over in my mind, making them even worse.

Oh, to be invisible!

Because I based my self-esteem on what others thought of me, unknowingly I gave them power to define my value. I wanted—needed—everyone to like me, so I became a people pleaser, trying to blend in. I didn't like myself, but I desperately wanted to believe that someone did.

From the time the abuse started I wanted to be invisible. I was quiet and very private—even with those closest to me. To avoid being hurt, mocked, or rejected, I rarely revealed my feelings or opinions.

Eventually, my desire for invisibility became so entrenched that I avoided getting out of my seat in class, even to sharpen my pencil or ask the teacher a question. I hated drawing attention to myself and even quit playing school sports because I didn't want people watching me. My dread of speaking or reading in front of others developed into a phobia that only worsened.

April 1991 (age 15)

I find myself believing in my daydreams so strongly that I get hurt and disappointed when reality hits me. My daydreams are very unrealistic. I know that, but it helps me escape.

In seventh grade, I remember, a teacher reprimanded me for talking to a friend in class. Tears ran down my face for the rest of the class period. I rarely talked anyway, so the shock of the reprimand (rejection) silenced me for a long time.

Isolation felt more comfortable than opening myself to the risk of trusting other people, but I paid a high price for safety and invisibility. I had a few friends, but not close ones. I rarely went out with them, preferring to stay home where it was safe. Social situations were too risky—no guarantees that I wouldn't face embarrassment, rejection, or criticism.

I feared exposing my true feelings because if anyone saw the pit of shame within me, they would surely be as disgusted by me as I was by myself. So I hid in the darkness, fearful of what the light might reveal.

Deaden the pain, deaden the emotions

I later learned I was developing predictable ways of dealing with the stress of maintaining two lives. Victims of abuse unconsciously use defense mechanisms to survive, to protect themselves from emotional pain. There was no way my young mind could feel the full extent of my terror, rage, and hurt and still function normally. But as I repressed the ugly memories and feelings, positive ones submerged as well. I became numb to all feelings in my attempt to avoid facing pain.

Over the years there were times when the memories came back and I consciously suppressed them—blocked them from my mind. If I refused to think about or acknowledge them, I could keep them under control. I believed that the memories of the past had no relevance to the present.

I rarely smiled, laughed, or cried, and when I did, it never came from deep inside. Shame and embarrassment might trigger tears, but emotions such as sadness or joy wouldn't. The fact that I don't remember crying during or after my abuse could mean that I immediately disengaged from my feelings. Tears seldom came when I wanted them to. I felt so bad when, at age eight, I couldn't cry at my beloved grandfather's funeral. I wondered why. I know now that had I opened the gate, a flood of other emotions could have poured out along with the sadness over my grandfather's death.

During those eight years of silence other defense mechanisms also came to my rescue. At times, in denial, I tried to convince myself the abuse never happened, that it was a dream.

Often I rationalized. Desperately wanting to believe that what Walter did was okay, I tried to justify his behavior (e.g., that Walter was putting medicine on me). Rationalizing his actions was easier than accepting the horror of what he did. Yet a little voice kept telling me that if his intentions were good I wouldn't feel so dirty every time the memory roared back to life.

As I grew older I often minimized what he did, telling myself, *he only touched me. It wasn't as if he raped me.* Yet the memories continued to plague me.

Some victims talk about "splitting" from the body at the time of the abuse in an effort to protect the mind and spirit. In my case, I endured the trauma itself by pretending I was asleep. I describe my splitting as "daydreaming," forcing my mind to concentrate on anything other than what was happening to my body. It wasn't safe to be connected to the "aware" part of me. Often, for hours a day I'd enter a fantasy world, dreaming about the future, which represented hope—something I was running out of.

I also coped by "splitting" the man who was like a grandfather to me from the man who molested me. My little-girl mind couldn't comprehend that the man who substituted for my grandfather on Grandparents' Day at school could be the same person as the man who did this ugly thing to me.

Protective shell

Later, even as the memories and emotions started to trickle into my consciousness, I still felt dead and empty inside. I developed a hardened exterior, keeping emotionally out of reach and inaccessible to the world.

One of the main ways I coped was by pushing away anyone who dared come too close. I distanced myself from most people and social situations. Walter had betrayed me, so the risk of trusting anyone else was too great. Keeping people at arm's length was better than letting them see the worthless, bad person I thought I was. Within the protective shell that became my own prison I lived a safe but lonely existence, longing for the one thing too risky to pursue— close relationships.

Living for safety and self-protection zapped the joy of living out of me. When I look at pictures of myself back then, I'm amazed at the lifeless person I see. My posture reflected the self-contempt I tried to hide. My shoulders slouched and my head hung in defeat. My eyes no longer sparkled and danced. The flickering light had been snuffed out, replaced by a faraway, disconnected look.

One day one of my classmates said, "Christa, why don't you ever look me in the eye when we're talking?" I didn't even realize that was something I should do. From that day on, however, whenever I talked with people I fought my habit of looking at the floor and determined to develop a new habit of confidently looking them in the eye. That was a great victory and a sign of hope.

Beyond survival

The more I learn, the more amazed I am at the ways the human mind can help victims escape from the pain. We repress, deny, rationalize, minimize, wish, and withdraw until the abuse lurks in the dim corners of the mind. Perry Draper writes, "The mind builds a defensive wall around the wounds of life so that we are able to go on without being totally devastated. Just as the body can build a protection around a flesh wound and continue to function even though the offending foreign body still remains under the skin, so the mind has ways to erect a wall of defense against threatening intrusions into our inner self."[2]

Yet buried feelings and memories are alive, not dead, and they eventually surface. Defense mechanisms are not permanent solutions. Although they can comfort for a while, they eventually imprison us. My defenses kept the terror and despair at bay, but they also destroyed my excitement for life and the joy of relating to other people.

There comes a time when we must let go of what helped us survive and discover how to truly live. The path to freedom leads straight through the pain, not away from it. Yet victims face a great battle when they refuse to deaden their souls any longer to the agony.

The irony is that anyone who fights to avoid pain will only continue to live with it. To fully embrace life, we need to first embrace the pain. Denying it leads to emotional and spiritual death.

Pain isn't necessarily a bad thing. It tells us that something needs attention. For example, if I have a toothache, I admit that it hurts, go to the dentist, and find out what the problem is. The dentist fixes it and the ache goes away. Yet if I were to deny the problem and avoid going to the dentist, my suffering would only increase as the problem worsened. The same holds true for emotional pain. Denying the truth prolongs our agony. Pain doesn't go away just because we haven't thought about it for a long time. It festers. It thwarts our growth—until we bring it to the light.

Searching out the hidden

We don't have to recall all the memories of the abuse before we can pursue healing. For some that will never happen. I remember only the first incident clearly and keenly sense it was a pattern for the rest. God allowed me to remember what I needed to, so that my healing could begin.

About the time I was in seventh grade, my defenses slowly began to release their iron grip, opening the gate to my subconscious. The truth seeped into my conscious mind.

I began having nightmares—the same one every time: I was walking down a steep staircase into a very dark room. Something—either in that room or chasing me— was so horrifying that before I could identify it I woke up, my heart pounding. Even in sleep, my memories haunted me. I now know these nightmares were messages from my subconscious, telling me I needed to deal with some things hidden there.

A "monster" terrified me when I was sleeping, and memories of Walter invaded my mind when I was awake. I didn't realize they were one and the same.

Pain is God's warning signal that something needs to be brought to the Healer. He wants to help us face the truth. He wants to carry us through it all. God desires wholeness for us, yet He cannot heal the parts of ourselves that we deny exist. Letting go of our protection may seem impossible, but it is fundamental to healing.

What to do if a someone tells you he or she has been sexually abused

1. Listen to what happened without questioning the person's memory, feelings, or integrity. Children seldom lie about acts of sexual exploitation. Telling is a huge risk, so the slightest hint of disbelief may make it nearly impossible for them to open up again.

2. Keep open lines of communication with the child. Victims who feel you are sympathetic, understanding, supportive, and optimistic will likely feel more comfortable making additional disclosures and discussing subsequent fears and troublesome feelings.

3. Show appropriate physical affection, and express your love. Avoid challenges, such as "Why didn't you tell me this before?" or "Why did you let it happen?" Give positive messages such as "I'm proud of you for telling me this," or "I know you couldn't help it." The child often fears punishment or the loss of the parents' love.

4. Don't minimize the experience, criticize, or hint at any punishment or blame for victims. They have endured enough already.

5. Emphasize that the child did nothing wrong. Victims need reassurances to calm their fears and guilt that they were somehow to blame for what happened.

6. Support the child's decision to tell the story. Don't ask victims to forget about abuse or not tell anyone. The truth is painful, but prohibiting further mention of the abuse slowly destroys the person who has already suffered much.

7. Report suspected abuse at once to the state agency responsible for investigating abuse. You cannot get into trouble even if your suspicions prove unfounded as long as you make the report in good faith. You can call ChildHelp USA for the number of the appropriate agency to call in your area. Their toll-free hotline number is (800) 422-4453.

8. Respect the victim's privacy. Be careful not to discuss the incidents in front of people who do not need to know what happened.

9. If you're the parent, keep your own feelings about the abuse separate from the child's. Find someone trustworthy with whom you can unburden yourself rather than worrying the victim about your well-being.

10. Try to maintain a calm, stable environment and resume as normal a life as possible. Protect the child but don't make him or her feel "singled out."

(The above was adapted from two brochures: "Just in Case. . . : Parental guidelines in case your child might someday be the victim of sexual abuse or exploitation," published by the *National Center for Missing & Exploited Children,* 1985; and *Talking About Child Sexual Abuse* [second edition] by Cornelia Spelman, published by the National Committee to Prevent Child Abuse, 1985, pp. 10-11, 15.)

Indications of possible sexual abuse[3]

- abrupt changes in behavior

- excessive anxiety: crying for no apparent reason, sleeplessness, nightmares, bed-wetting, loss of appetite, depression

- withdrawal, regression to childish behavior

- difficulty at school: behavioral problems, inability to concentrate, drop in grades, absenteeism

- aggressive behavior: irritability, hostility, disruptive behaviors, defiance of authority figures

- self-destructive behavior: abuse of alcohol or drugs, self-mutilation, attempted suicide, theft, promiscuity, prostitution, running away

- seductive behavior: acting out sexual behaviors inappropriate to the child's age

- indirect messages: coded communication in which the adult must listen for what is not said. For example, if a child says, "I don't want to stay with——," he or she may be trying to tell about sexual abuse.

- physical symptoms: psychosomatic illnesses such as stomachaches, irritation of the mouth, genital, or anal areas; venereal disease.

[1]E. Sue Blume, *Secret Survivors* (New York: Ballantine Books, 1990) p. 113.

[2]Perry L. Draper, *Haunted Memories* (Grand Rapids: Fleming H. Revell, 1996), p. 35.

[3]The Illusion Theater Prevention Program, Minneapolis, MN.

Take me, Lord—take me now
I want to lie down and die
I can't share my feelings
I feel empty inside
My life is a mess
I can't understand why.

Give me life or give me death
The decision is up to me
But what I choose is a direct reflection
Of what I think my life will be.

Christa Sands

CHAPTER 3

Silent Cries

O my God, I cry out by day, but you do not answer,
by night, and am not silent.
Do not be far from me, for trouble is near
and there is no one to help.

Psalm 22:2, 11

The poem on the opposite page is part of a longer one I wrote in junior high. As memories of the abuse started creeping back into my mind, things became worse before they got better. The memories dredged up emotions I couldn't deal with—rage, shame, humiliation.

I tried to silently endure, but I grew increasingly withdrawn, depressed, and emotional. And no one seemed to notice. Tears flowed nearly every day. At school I often

January 1991 (age 14)

Right now I'm sitting on my bed contemplating suicide. Of course, I don't actually want to die. I'll just take enough pills so people will realize I have a serious problem. I just want people to care. I feel so alone, like there's no one who will listen.

From the looks of things now, it doesn't seem like I'll ever be truly happy. I had so many dreams, but they are all fading fast. I'm scared I'll feel like this forever. I don't see the point of going on.

had to hide in the bathroom till I could regain control. I didn't understand it, but all of a sudden tears sprang up like an artesian well—tears I couldn't shed before. Yet God was keeping track of them all. I know now that He truly does care. Psalm 56:8 says, "Record my lament; list my tears on your scroll—are they not in your record?"

Umbrella of sadness

I thought about the abuse constantly and sank into a deep depression that lasted for months. Huddled under an ever-present umbrella of sadness, I wondered if I would ever feel joy again. My sleeping patterns changed, and although I slept most of the time, I still battled fatigue, irritability, and moodiness. I no longer cared about my appearance. Struggles with motivation and concentration left me behind in my class work. I often stayed home from school or went home "sick."

Consumed with my own ordeal, I became enraged inside when I saw others get upset over "minor problems."

I wanted to scream, "How can you get so upset over these little things when I am trying to decide if life is worth living?" But I held my rage, like everything else, inside.

At home, parental lectures about my unwillingness to join the family prompted more tears of sadness, loneliness, and anger. During vacations with relatives I spent my time alone in the woods, the cabin, or the van, barely saying a word to anyone. Neither my parents nor other relatives understood why. They apparently thought I was a typical teenager giving her parents a hard time.

If ever in my life I needed people to wrap their arms around me and tell me everything was going to be okay, this was it. But I couldn't tell them what I needed. Though people noticed changes in me, they didn't realize they were silent cries for help. My mother, especially, is such a trusting person that it never dawned on her that my withdrawal could have signaled something as horrid as sexual abuse from a family friend.

Suicidal thoughts

I would walk the halls at school alone, not a part of the weekend plans, secrets, or joking around. The laughter I heard haunted me because I desperately wanted to feel joy again. For everyone else, life went on as usual while for me it seemed to be unwinding—slowing to a stop. I kept envisioning myself falling down a pit, wondering when I was going to hit bottom and start climbing up again, hoping life was going to get better. I kept asking myself, *Why doesn't anyone care?*

I admit I became an expert at wearing masks and pretending everything was fine, even though I was drowning in a sea of pain. I know now that people did care about me, but back then I brushed away anyone who tried to find out what was wrong. The more I isolated myself, the more I desperately needed someone to rescue me.

Hope—the one thing that had kept me going through my darkest days—had vanished. Without it I had nothing. "When I hoped for good," Job wrote, "evil came; when I looked for light, then came darkness. The churning inside me never stops" (Job 30:26–27). I needed something to

TEEN SUICIDE CRISIS

- Every 78 seconds another teenager attempts suicide.
- In 1995, 1 in 12 high school students attempted suicide and 24 percent seriously considered it.
- Suicide is the third leading cause of death among adolescents.
- Since 1950 the teen suicide rate has increased by more than 400 percent.

grasp, but everything was crumbling around me. The past was too painful to look back on, the present—as truth reared its ugly head—became too torturous to look at, and the future offered nothing to look forward to. Suicide seemed the only answer.

Every day on the bus ride to and from school, I daydreamed about my suicide and funeral. Sometimes I truly did want to die; other times I only wanted people to know the intensity of what I was going though. Either way, I wanted my pain to end. Sometimes I envisioned someone bursting in the door just as I was going to kill myself, saving me from my fate. This was unrealistic, but I desperately wanted someone to care and help me survive.

At one point I told some of my friends how depressed I was, and they made a joke out of it. Later, when I told my parents I wanted to kill myself, they were very concerned but didn't pursue getting help for me. No one could fathom a girl like me living such an emotional nightmare.

I believed Satan's lie that no one cared about me, so it wouldn't matter if I died. Satan pursued me, and his lies drowned out the truth (Psalm 143:3–4).

Spiritual withdrawal

Lonely and isolated in the dark pit, I longed for someone to bring me light. But everyone seemed just out of my grasp, including God. I had accepted Jesus as my Savior not long before the abuse began. Though I believed in God, I relied on my parents' faith rather than building my own solid relationship with Him. My young mind could have deduced that God didn't love me because He "rewarded" my profession of faith by allowing Walter to abuse me. But God protected me from totally rejecting Him in anger.

Blessed with a rich heritage of faith, I had strong spiritual roots, but questions of why God permitted the abuse hung like a heavy curtain in the back of my mind. When my very life depended on receiving the love and comfort I'd heard so much about in Sunday school, I sensed a barrier between God and me. I neither felt His presence nor found His comfort. If God had turned His back on me, hope seemed impossible.

For a while I rebelled against my parents' solid faith. I remember many fights in which I would scream at Mom and Dad until I became hoarse because I felt they were forcing me to go to church, youth group, or other church-related activities. I prayed so many times, but I received no answers—at least not the way I expected. His silence was deafening.

Satan whispered lies, telling me I didn't deserve God's healing and love—and I believed him. Feelings of abandonment seemed to take up permanent residence in my soul. The darkness, growing blacker and blacker, became my "closest friend" (Psalm 88:18). My meager faith quickly turned to quicksand as I sank further into the pit.

My doubts of God's power and love intensified into doubts of His very existence. The God I could not see became the God I could not hear or trust. Yet, in my despair, I continued to call out for mercy. I later learned that God doesn't want us to hide our doubt and despair beneath false words and feelings. He wants us to express them honestly. David did when he wrote this: "How long, O LORD? Will you forget me forever? How long will you hide your face from me? How long must I wrestle with my thoughts and every day have sorrow in my heart? How long will my enemy triumph over me?" (Psalm 13:1–2).

We need to be open about the pain from our past and our anger at God for not immediately taking it away. An open relationship with God is essential to healing.

Breaking the silence

Even as a part of me wanted to give up and die, part of me wanted to fight and truly live, not just survive. I believed there was more to life than this deadness. An emotional wreck, I realized that if I wanted help, I had to open up and tell my parents. The secret was like a poison destroying me. I wanted to scream the truth to the world. Inside myself I did.

> *And then the day came*
> *when the risk to remain*
> *tight in a bud*
> *was more painful*
> *than the risk*
> *it took to blossom.*
> —AUTHOR UNKNOWN

But after mastering silence—my friend and protector—for so long, I had no idea how to break free from its imprisonment.

David described similar agony for not confessing sin: "When I was silent and still, not even saying anything good, my anguish increased" (Psalm 39:2). Only when we acknowledge and confess sin—including sin done to us—do we find freedom.

Denial no longer worked. I knew the abuse happened and it had affected me deeply. I knew Walter did something wrong, but if I could just find the right word to name the evil maybe I could make someone understand. A dictionary search only left me further confused: abuse? rape? assault? molestation? harassment?

I couldn't imagine living the rest of my life in this personal hell, so I decided I had to talk to my parents. I still feared they wouldn't believe me over their friend, and I was petrified of what Walter might do to me if I told (though he had never threatened me). But I had to take the risk.

After many sleepless nights, I formulated a number of plans for telling my parents. I even tried to think of other adults who might help me tell them. Yet fears of worst-case scenarios and ridicule filled my mind. Finally mustering the courage, I asked my mom if I could see a counselor.

She didn't understand the depth of my pain. "Why don't you talk to our pastor first?" she suggested.

My heart sank. I was scared to talk to anyone close to my parents. At that point I believed I had only two options: tell my parents myself or attempt suicide so I could get help.

I now know that suicide is a permanent solution to a temporary problem. There are always other choices. Suicide should never be an option—period.

A caring stranger

One night, when I was fifteen, I was watching television, and a number for a teen crisis hotline appeared on the screen. This was my answer. It took a tremendous amount of courage, but I dialed the number and told a stranger my deepest pain. Afterward, I wrote in my journal:

February 13, 1991 (age 15)

Right now I am literally shaking. I just got off the phone with an extremely caring stranger who is a volunteer for a crisis hotline. After eight years, I finally told my secret to someone I'd never met and probably never will. I feel relieved, in a way, that I told someone, but I'm also scared that people I know will find out. As I was talking, I shook with a rush of emotions—shame, hurt, embarrassment, and anger. The lady on the phone told me I had been sexually abused and that what Walter did was wrong and not my fault. It's wonderful to finally know the name of what happened to me. She thinks I should tell my parents. I don't know. Right now that thought frightens me. I wish I could tell them so I can work through this and get on with my life. I want to work toward my dreams and build better friendships, but I feel my secret is blocking my path. It is strange having someone know my secret after so many years.

Having reached the bottom of the pit I had envisioned myself falling down, I decided to risk telling my secret in hopes of finding the light, even if it meant going through a lot of pain first. But from the time I made the hotline call it literally took me months to build up my courage.

The memory of finally telling my mom and dad will always be engraved on my mind. I had come home from being out with friends yet feeling very depressed. I sat down and made a list of reasons why I should and should not tell my parents:

TELL:	NOT TELL:
• better relationships with parents, relatives, friends	• only one reason: they might not believe me
• get help from a counselor	
• feel more comfortable with males	
• find justice	

The biggest risk of my life

The time had come. Terrified, I gathered all my strength, sat my parents down, and first asked them to

> Healing: "Change from the helpless and
> hurting victim to a mature person
> who is able, with the help of God,
> to face with honesty, courage, and faith
> whatever life may bring."
>
> PERRY L. DRAPER

read my diary entry about the crisis hotline phone call. I felt I was taking the biggest risk of my life. I felt degraded. Shame coursed through my body as I tried to find words to explain what had happened to me so many years before. This was the hardest thing I had ever done.

By the time I finished, I was crying hard in Dad's arms, and Mom was holding my hand. "You believe me?" I asked, incredulously.

"Of course," Dad assured me. "We'll always believe our own daughter over someone else!"

What a tremendous relief! I finally had the support I'd needed for so long. I had spoken the truth, brought it into the light, and begun the long journey of healing and wholeness, which never could have occurred had I chosen to stay in the prison of silence.

I cannot imagine what my mom and dad were feeling as I told them their trusted friend had sexually abused me. I know they later felt guilt, but it never crossed their minds that they needed to protect their daughter from Walter. And I know they also struggled with anger that such a good friend could do this. My mother went through a period of depression during which she cried all the time. I think she blamed herself for not seeing signs of what was happening.

Abuse always leaves more than one victim in its wake. The whole family suffers. And when the abuser is part of the victim's family, the confusion and betrayal of trust are far worse.

A vital support team

Thoreau once said, "It takes two to tell the truth: one to say it and another to hear it." A listener's reaction often determines how successfully a victim navigates the healing process. The three greatest things a person can do for sexual abuse victims are these:

- listen to them
- believe their story
- care about them.

March 17, 1991 (age 15)

I did it—I really did it! After eight years of silence, I finally told my parents! Mom and I cried as I told them some of the memories of what happened to me. Dad went to talk to a friend about what we should do next. Mom and I talked for a long time afterward. I feel a glimmer of hope. After climbing that hill I face a mountain. But hopefully there are lots of rewards once I reach the top.

And don't give the slightest hint of questioning their memory, feelings, or integrity. Rejection or denial can be as traumatic as the abuse itself.

> The God of all grace, who called you to his eternal glory in Christ, after you have suffered a little while, will himself restore you and make you strong, firm and steadfast.
>
> 1 PETER 5:10

I owe much of the success of my healing journey to the fact that my parents supported and cared for me every step of the way. They did not sweep the abuse under the rug, as tempting as that may have been. We have maintained open communication, talking about issues as needed. And, with my permission, they have discussed with friends and family how the abuse has affected all of us.

Even those who may not have a supportive environment can still find healing, however. The Lord Jesus Christ invites each of us to reach out to Him for support and care. "Come to me," Jesus says, "and I will give you rest. Take my yoke upon you and learn from me, for I am gentle and humble in heart . . . . My yoke is easy and my burden is light" (Matthew 11:28–29).

I never understood these verses until someone explained that a yoke is a wooden frame that binds two oxen together so they can work as one strong unit in the field. In this verse, Jesus is saying, "Take my yoke. Unite with me. Together we will journey through life, and I will help you through whatever comes your way." Facing life alone increases despair and hopelessness. Facing life with Christ at your side, yoked together with you, prepares your heart for a harvest of peace, rest, and joy—even in the midst of trials.

SIGNS OF DEPRESSION

- significant change in mood or behavior, such as change in eating, sleeping, or personal hygiene habits
- loss of interest in pleasurable activities
- ongoing feelings of sadness, discouragement, or hopelessness
- diminished ability to think or concentrate
- fatigue, loss of energy, inactivity, and boredom
- recurring absences from school and/or decrease in school performance
- recurring physical illnesses such as headaches and stomachaches
- increased irritability and/or moodiness
- decline in self-esteem, feelings of worthlessness
- unexplained or excessive tearfulness
- suicidal thoughts

For a while it was hard for me to understand why those around me didn't notice the depression, cries for help, and other disturbing signs. Now I realize that each person saw only one or two pieces of the puzzle. My friends saw the spontaneous crying and heard me admit feeling depressed. My teachers saw the withdrawal. My relatives saw my moodiness and difficulty submitting to authority. My parents saw my sleeping patterns change and heard me say I didn't want to go to Walter's house anymore. If each person had shared his or her piece of the puzzle, together they would have come up with a picture of my inner turmoil.

Family and friends play a vital role in the healing process. Victims start their healing journey by speaking the truth, but deaf ears, ignorance, or uncaring hearts can abruptly block it. Those with compassion and a willingness to hear the painful truth can unlock the prison of silence so the victims can begin the journey toward freedom and wholeness.

Reminders for parents

1. Develop strong, open, and loving relationships with your children. Make time to be involved in their lives, to help meet their emotional needs as well as their physical needs. Abusers target emotionally needy kids desperate for someone to fill their emptiness with "love" and attention. If parents don't fill this need at home, children are vulnerable to offers of friendship from people who may not be safe.

2. Don't believe the dangerous myth, however, that abuse doesn't happen in solid Christian families. To do so only perpetuates the vicious cycle of silence. Abuse can and does happen in families with healthy parent-child relationships.

3. Don't assume that your children would tell you if they were ever abused.

    a. Because most abusers are known to both the child and the parents, children think their parents wouldn't believed them rather than an adult, especially if the abuser is in their own family.

    b. Children often blame themselves and fear repercussions from their parents or the abuser.

c. The paralyzing shame of abuse can silence victims who may otherwise have a healthy relationship with their parents and others.

4. Don't be overly suspicious, but monitor your children's friendships with adults and adolescents. A potentially dangerous friendship may appear innocent to begin with, but a child can become so emotionally dependent on an abuser that the child can do little when the abusive behavior begins. Abusers have a keen sense of children's weaknesses and will take advantage of them, destroying the child's innocence.

5. Victims need at least one healthy, caring, supportive relationship for healing to take place. Clinical psychologist Dr. John Townsend writes, "Darkness always needs the light of unconditional love to give up its secrets." It is in a relationship that abuse victims are hurt and betrayed, and it will be through relationships that they will find healing.

Warning signs that a person may be considering suicide

- violent behavior and/or recurring accidents
- suicide threats and/or talking about death
- giving away favorite possessions, getting life in order
- withdrawal from family and friends
- drug and alcohol abuse
- experiencing a recent traumatic event, such as the loss of a parent, friend, or love relationship
- previous suicide attempts
- prolonged depression, or becoming abruptly happy after a period of depression

What to do if you suspect someone is contemplating suicide

- Take seriously all threats of suicide or even casual conversation about it. But also be aware that the more specific the plan, the greater the risk. Encourage the person to talk about what's bothering him or her. Reassure him or her that you will listen. To dismiss suicide threats as merely attention seeking is to gamble with the life of someone you love.

- Never promise to keep suicidal intentions a secret. Take responsibility to assist the person in finding the help needed.

- Ask feeling-oriented questions. Say, for example, "Have your problems been getting you down so much that you're thinking of harming yourself?" Remember: Most people don't want to die. They only want to end the pain.

- Be firm. Don't ask people who are suicidal what they'd like to do. Tell them what they must do. They must seek help. Urge them to call a local crisis hotline or the toll-free ChildHelp USA national hotline: (800) 422-4453.

- Reassure the suicidal person that depression and suicidal tendencies can be treated. Don't lecture or point out all the reasons the person has for living. It doesn't help.

- Don't try to counsel the suicidal person by yourself. Help the individual connect with trained clergy, Christian counselors, therapists, or mental health professionals. Caring for and supporting the emo-tionally wounded is just as important, if not more so, as it is for the physically wounded. When people have been physically injured, it's easy to see their need. Wounded hearts and souls are invisible, however, though their pain is no less real or agonizing. "A man's spirit sustains him in sickness, but a crushed spirit who can bear?" (Proverbs 18:14).

• Check with a doctor for possible physical causes for the depression—chemical imbalance, drug interac-tion, etc.

• Show unconditional love in both words and action. Show physical affection freely. Many people who are suicidal prefer to live if they can receive understand-ing and support from family and friends.

If you have been sexually abused, call the toll-free ChildHelp USA national hotline: (800) 422-4453.

CHAPTER **4**

Facing the Truth

Let the morning bring me word of your unfailing love,
for I have put my trust in you.
Show me the way I should go,
for to you I lift up my soul . . .
may your good Spirit lead me on level ground.
Psalm 143:8–10

Naively I thought that as soon as I told my parents, my abuser would be whisked off to jail, newspapers would carry the story, everyone in the community would learn about it, and life for me would get better.

That's what I thought I wanted to happen. But when my parents sought advice regarding what to do next, surprisingly I became anxious. I felt humiliated. When no one knew about the abuse, I wanted to shout it from the rooftops. Yet when a few people found out, I wanted to hide.

I'm thankful my parents reported the abuse, however, because most parents don't—either out of denial or from fear of public exposure.

When the day came for me to meet with a deputy sheriff and a social services representative, I had no idea what to expect. I grew increasingly anxious and nervous as Mom and I drove into town. The idea of telling strangers my most personal experience scared me—especially since the deputy was a man.

For the record

When we arrived, the compassion in the eyes of both of them eased my fears. We all introduced ourselves, and I immediately liked Wanda, the woman from social services. "Mrs. Sands," she said to my mother, "we'd like to try talking to Christa alone first."

Mom nodded.

"Do you want some water?" Wanda asked me. I could tell she wanted to make this as easy for me as possible.

I shook my head. I was so nervous I couldn't even think of drinking anything. My heart pounded as I followed her and the deputy into a small office and sat down, shaking. As Wanda closed the door, tears sprang to my eyes and ran down my face. I hadn't uttered a word yet, but all the pain—buried so long—now erupted.

The deputy explained that they would tape-record the conversation and then transcribe it for the record.

Grabbing a tissue from my purse, I dabbed at my eyes, trying to force myself to stop crying. It was useless. Wanda called my mom into the room for moral support.

The deputy turned the tape recorder on, then stated the date, time, and the names of those present. Both he and Wanda asked me questions—first easy ones, then tougher ones. I told them exactly what happened, answering the

REALITIES OF PROSECUTION

- A sex offender who assaults an adult is four times more likely to receive a prison term than one who attacks a child.

- Of all those assaulting children, 1 in 100 is apprehended.

- Of all those apprehended, 1 in 10 is convicted.

- Of all those convicted
    60% are released on probation and serve no sentence.
    26% are sent to state mental hospitals for treatment.
    14% are sentenced to prison.

- The average time convicted molesters spend in mental health facilities is 18 months.

- The average time convicted molesters spend in prison is 41 months.

- Calculated from the statistics above, each molester spends an average of 15.09 minutes in jail.

From the brochure *In Defense of Children,* produced in cooperation with Societies League Against Molestation (SLAM) and the Help Find Johnny Gosch group of West Des Moines, Iowa.

when, where, and how. *If only someone could answer the why,* I thought. Then they asked me if I thought Walter had molested my brother. As far as we knew, he hadn't. He displayed none of the symptoms.

Some questions brought waves of shame, but my interviewers' caring attitudes helped me a lot. *If everyone else in town finds out,* I thought, *I hope they're half as nice about it as these people are.*

After the deputy turned off the tape recorder, he tapped his pen on the desk. "We've compiled a list of other families Walter has baby-sat for in the past," he told us, "and we're going to talk to them, too. But no one will know who initiated the investigation—not even Walter."

Wanda leaned forward. "We're also following up on reports that he has abused other children."

Inwardly I seethed at the thought that I probably wasn't the first or the last. "If only I had told Mom and Dad right away the first time it happened . . ." I sniffled. "Maybe I could have saved other kids a lot of pain."

Wanda reached over and patted my hand. "You should be proud you came forward at all," she said.

Both she and the deputy told me to call them any time I had questions, wanted an update on the investigation, or just needed to talk. I appreciated their kindness. The interview wasn't nearly as bad as I'd feared, but I realized how difficult it is to talk about being sexually abused. I thought about it all the time, but publicly telling the details humiliated me. I felt filthy. It would have been easier to deny my pain, yet I didn't want to live in a silent prison forever. Speaking up was the only way to diminish the power shame held over me.

As it was, two years passed before I could tell friends and other relatives about the abuse. In silence shame grows like a weed. Until we expose the root, the abuse itself, we can never fulfill what God desires for each of us.

The question of prosecution

As the investigation continued, I had to decide whether to prosecute or not. We had little doubt that Walter had abused others and would continue to hurt innocent children if no one intervened. Perpetrators usually don't quit on their own. During his or her lifetime the average offender, without intervention, may abuse as many as one hundred children. I wanted to stop Walter and make sure he got help.

June 1991 (age 15)

I am outraged that rumors have abounded for years that Walter likes little girls. Apparently his "problem" has been fairly common knowledge, yet no one bothered to tell the authorities. I am appalled that respected community leaders suspected something, but no one dared get involved. The authorities were in the dark until I came forward.

The statute of limitations actually ran out before I reported the abuse, but we learned that we might be able to take advantage of some loopholes to build a case. I was petrified, though, of facing him in court and having to answer difficult, embarrassing questions in public.

I'm thankful my parents helped weigh the pros and cons yet left the final decision up to me. I would have felt powerless again had the decision been made for me. As much as I wanted to keep Walter from abusing more children, I wasn't strong enough to pursue prosecution. I still wonder if I made the right decision.

Children, teens, and adults who do testify against their abusers demonstrate raw courage. Testifying is an incredibly painful process, yet for some it facilitates healing. But how sad that children should even have to think of prosecuting an adult.

Can't anyone stop him?

I started seeing Marie, a counselor, almost every week for five months. Again, naively, I thought that if I told my parents and started getting counseling, I'd be healed in a month, life would stop being a burden, and I would miraculously emerge from my protective shell. It didn't work that way.

One day, while I was waiting to see Marie, she came out of her office with a grim look on her face. "Your dad just called," she said.

Right away I knew why. My heart started beating fast, and my whole body tensed. I glanced at my mom.

Marie motioned to us. "Why don't you both come in and we'll talk about it."

I sat stiffly in her office and listened as she relayed Dad's update on the investigation. The officers had talked to Walter, and he denied everything. My emotions rollercoastered from surprise to fear to relief: I hadn't known exactly when they planned to talk to him. I feared what he might do to me. And I was glad he finally knew his secret wasn't a secret anymore.

But there was something else. Apparently, in interviews throughout the community, the only thing people said was that they had heard rumors or they felt uncomfortable around him. How could people accept Walter's "problem" and do nothing to stop it?

The rest of the counseling session was a blur. I spent the whole hour blinking back tears. My chest ached from emotions waiting, needing, to surface. Afterward, I fled to the safety of the car and surrendered to a violent flood of tears. Oh, the incredible, terrifying pain!

Later that week Mom and I met again with Wanda from social services and learned, among other things, that the authorities had interviewed eight families Walter babysat for. Again, all they admitted was that they had heard rumors.

I couldn't stand it. Trembling, I asked, "Do you think it would help anyone else come forward if I wrote my story and went public with it?"

"It might." Wanda sounded hopeful. "If you're willing to do it, I'll help you get it published in the newspaper."

As we were about to leave her office, I smiled and she gently took my arm. "It's nice to see you smile," she said. "Last time I saw you it was pretty traumatic."

For some reason that gave me hope.

Looking for a miracle

When I began counseling, I expected an instant miracle, and I felt disappointed when I didn't get one. But I couldn't expect to change deeply ingrained beliefs and behaviors so quickly.

God does have the power to heal instantly, but I believe He most often works His miracle of emotional healing over time. Our character is refined as we persevere through pain. It was very difficult, but I had to learn to be patient in order to see God heal the deepest parts of me.

The healing journey often feels more like a war zone than the path toward wholeness. I remember many times leaving my counselor's office, thinking my sessions were pointless. As far as I was concerned, I not only wasn't getting better, I was getting worse. But I felt that way

May 1991 (age 15)

Today my teacher called on me to tell the class what the word "stale" meant. For some reason I couldn't find the words to express the meaning. Moments dragged on. I thought he would ask someone else, but when he didn't, I finally said I didn't know. "I find that hard to believe," he said.

Then he told me I should "reach out" more. The silence of my classmates, as well as his tone of voice made me feel stupid, embarrassed, and out of place. The words "reach out" stung. They pushed to the surface my hidden pain of being abused. As tears ran down my cheeks, I bent my head in shame and wiped each one away. I don't think anyone noticed. No one ever notices.

I wanted to scream, "Don't you think I want to?" I can't, though. I just can't.

because, for the first time, I was facing the horror of the abuse and feeling all the pain I had stuffed inside so long. Often I wanted to give up, but something inside me refused to quit fighting. I wanted more out of life than a prison of fear, shame, and insecurity.

When the Enemy strikes, we have two choices:

1. Fight the battles that lead to freedom, or
2. Passively allow the Enemy to take us captive and then endure a life of bondage.

Taking three steps forward and two steps back can be frustrating, but with persistence and determination we can keep making progress.

A friend of mine, also a sexual abuse victim, once wrote to me, describing the healing process from her perspective:

> The pain seems only to [come] harder and harder, not easier and easier. I don't want to fight anymore, but if I don't, then [my abuser] wins. Life is so short. We shouldn't have to spend so much of it dealing with something that wasn't our fault. It's not fair! Many times I'm almost ready to give up. Yet when I look at you and see how much you've struggled with this and how much you've accomplished, I can't help but push a little harder. So help me, this is one battle I won't lose. But I am scared, and I feel very alone. I just hope God doesn't allow this to do me in.

How grateful I was that someone had already bene-fitted from what God was teaching me!

The healing spiral

People often describe the healing process as a spiral. We must face the same issues again and again as we integrate new life experiences into our healing. Yet each time we face them, pain's grip on us weakens a little more, and we can see things from a new perspective.

Sometimes issues I think I've already laid to rest come to life again several weeks, months, or even years later. My journals capture this yo-yo effect.

As we continue to work through these issues and feelings, though, gradually the good days outnumber the bad, changes become more evident, and the pain doesn't consume every waking moment. We begin to feel freedom, maybe even joy. We can move on in victory, the past only a dim precursor to the growth we now see.

Asking for help

Though I didn't realize it until years later, taking the initiative to tell my parents was the first step toward my own healing. The abuse taught me to be passive, to think I could do little to change anything. The breakthrough came when I quit being passive and admitted I was in pain, in need of help.

Many times Jesus offered healing to those who admitted their need. For example, John's gospel tells the story of a man who had been an invalid for 38 years. He waited by the Pool of Bethesda for someone to carry him to the supposed healing waters there (see John 5:1–15).

When Jesus walked by one day, He asked the man, "Do you want to get well?"

The invalid wasn't passive. He had tried to get to the pool. And when Jesus healed him, he picked up his mat and walked off, living in the knowledge that Jesus had made him whole.

God reaches out to us, too, but He won't heal us if we neither want healing nor seek it. He invites us to admit our need and become active agents in our own healing process.

We can take a step of faith, believing that God, who loves us more than we can possibly imagine, will heal us and free us from the past. Or we can remain passive, hoping that someday we'll forget and the pain will go away (which never happens). The choice is up to us.

Victims believe only time will heal their wounds, but this myth is another form of denial. Unhealed wounds become infected. They can threaten life itself. And when victims wait many years to admit they were abused, imagine all the time and energy wasted, trying to keep the memories and pain away.

Author and abuse survivor Joyce Meyer writes, "People who are in prison function, but they are not free. However, sometimes prisoners—whether physical or emotional—become so accustomed to being in bondage that they settle in with their condition and learn to live with it."[1] God desires freedom for us—not just functioning—but we can't know that freedom when we're draining our energies by denying truth.

The Lord wanted to restore my life and make me whole even more than I wanted it for myself, but I had to take the first step. Once I actively pursued healing, He began working in me even though I didn't always realize the progress I was making.

Taking responsibility

Dr. John Townsend writes, "When we risk bringing part of ourselves into the light, we are 'owning,' or taking responsibility for, our lives."[2] God is the Ultimate Healer, but I learned there was work only I could do.

- I needed to tell my story. No one else could be my voice. This is part of my active role in the pursuit of wholeness.

- I also needed to identify some of my own choices that hurt me and other people. Healing will not happen when we use our past as an excuse for our behavior or refuse to take responsibility to change.

- I needed to take responsibility for the walls I continued to erect and hide behind. They served their purpose at one point, but in my own fear of vulnerability I had refused to dismantle them. And that only hindered my growth and healing.

- I had to take responsibility for words of anger I had spoken that hurt others and accomplished nothing. They may have stemmed from the abuse, but blaming the past for my actions didn't do any good, either.

- Though I wasn't to blame for the abuse, I also had to answer to God for my response to it and receive His forgiveness. I knew there were things I needed to change. I simply had to do it. No one else could change me.

- Taking responsibility also meant changing my mind-set from victim to survivor. Satan wants us to live as helpless victims, blaming the past for our present behavior. He doesn't want us to bring our pain to the Healer.

God will meet us if only we will take the first step. Making a conscious choice to accept healing allows God to supply the strength, determination, and courage to fight the battle ahead.

Reminders about emotional healing

- Recovery from emotional wounds requires patience. Endure.

- The healing process often seems like three steps forward, two steps back. Keep moving forward.

- Working through pain produces strong character. Persevere.

- The journey toward healing may feel more like a war zone than a path toward wholeness. Fight.

- You may often feel you're getting worse instead of better. Trust God for progress.

- Freedom from emotional bondage is worth the struggle. Don't give up.

Fight for the children: Help change inadequate laws. Call or write your local, state, and federal government officials and let your voice be heard on behalf of the victims:

1. Fight to lengthen the legal time limit for children and adolescents to report and prosecute sexual abusers. Victims need time to process what happened to them and heal from the abuse. It's not fair to force them to decide whether to prosecute or not—before they're strong enough to handle the repercussions—just because the statutes of limitations are quickly running out.

2. Fight for stiffer penalties for child abusers. Relatively speaking, punishment for perpetrators is little more than a slap on the wrist compared to the consequences for the abused children who may be left with a "life sentence" of mental, emotional, and spiritual pain.

[1]Joyce Meyer, *Beauty for Ashes: Receiving Emotional Healing* (Tulsa: Harrison House. 1994), p. 10.

[2]Dr. John Townsend, *Hiding From Love* (Grand Rapids: Zondervan, 1996), p. 185.

Years of suffering, tears of pain
Walls built to block pouring rain
Depression, anguish, utter despair
Wanting, needing someone to care
Will you ever see what you did?
How you affected this lonely kid?
Fierce strong emotions deep inside
Desperately seeking a place to hide.

Christa Sands

CHAPTER 5

Glimpses of Light

Do not gloat over me, my enemy!
Though I have fallen, I will rise.
Though I sit in darkness,
the Lord will be my light.

Micah 7:8

Soon after I told my parents about the abuse, I felt compelled to help other victims. In one of my first counseling sessions I told Marie how much I wanted to do this.

"I think for now, Christa," she said, "it would be better for you to concentrate on your own healing."

I felt hurt. She seemed so flippant about my need to care and help, but I gradually began to see the wisdom of her words. In my journal I wrote:

> Hopefully, someday I can help people go through
> the pain and joy of healing, but for now I must
> focus on my own journey.

I also had to put on hold my desire to publish my story in the newspaper. Wanda wanted to make sure I was emotionally ready to go public. "I think you need a safety net of supportive, caring people around you who can help you handle the public's reactions," she said. "There are bound to be some negative comments. It would be good if you could tell those closest to you what happened first— kind of practicing for the questions people may ask."

I knew it would be difficult to tell others because, at this point, I had told only my parents, Marie, Wanda, and the deputy. Writing is one thing, but saying the words out loud is quite another. My friends and relatives still didn't know about my abuse, and I knew I needed to tell them. But it took a long time to build up courage.

A guide along the path

Meanwhile, Marie became my guide, walking with me along the path to healing—offering advice, encouragement, and a listening ear. The best advice she gave me was to read as much as I could about sexual abuse to better understand the issues and the healing process. She also advised me to write down my thoughts and feelings as issues came up.

Reading about the pervasiveness of abuse and about other victims' feelings helped me feel less alone. I had already been journaling for several months. But in relating what I was learning to my own thoughts and emotions, writing proved therapeutic.

Early on, when Marie asked me to write down what I hoped our sessions would accomplish, I wrote:

1. I hope Walter gets help. Sometimes I wish he would get thrown in jail for the rest of his life. Yet it is important to me that he understands what he did to me and how it has affected my whole life. I want to handle my anger better and forgive Walter.

2. Through healing I hope to become a better person. I want to like myself. I hope I can open up more. I have a hard time reaching out to others, especially guys. I have a hard time trusting people. I don't go out at all with my friends. I call them "my friends" because they're the people I talk to, but there's no one I trust enough to tell what I'm going through. I really hope that changes soon.

3. I want to grow through this experience and become stronger. I hope I'll be able to get over the pain deep inside. I want to enjoy life and not have this black cloud hanging over my head.

Honest emotions

One of the first issues we talked about in counseling was my need to express feelings that had lain dormant for years but now were eating me up inside. After I told my parents about the abuse, I was totally unprepared for the flood of emotions boiling beneath the surface. Now I could literally feel in

May 1991 (age 15)

I thought that once I told my secret my parents would feel my pain and understand the intensity of what I'm going through. It's not like that, though. I can't transfer some of my pain into their bodies so that I won't have to deal with as much. It's a lonely thought that each person has to carry his burden alone with no one to comprehend the fullness of the pain. I desperately need someone to understand and care. I feel so hopeless. Suicide is an alternative I think of often.

my chest the anger, grief, and shame clamoring to come out.

Marie helped me see that recovery depended on my ability to attach names to my emotions and to express them. I couldn't let go of—or move past—what I couldn't feel. I tried to hide beneath a calm demeanor, scared that once I opened the floodgates I would be consumed by emotions like grief and anger. Yet I needed to be able to feel if I ever wanted to feel joy, to feel alive. That meant being honest with God and with other people about my emotions. I often pretended to be doing fine when I felt so hopeless inside.

I began to see Jesus as the best example of how to live authentically. He never masked His emotions: His frustration and anger, His tears of grief and sadness, or His deep agony and joy (see Matthew 21:12–13; Matthew 23:13–33, 37; John 11:14–36; Hebrews 12:2–3).

But as my emotions began to surface, I couldn't control them. I struggled to find balance between extremes.

Guilt awakened

My mind wrestled with what I could have done or should have done to stop the abuse. Why had I pretended to be asleep? I kicked myself for not "waking up" so Walter would know I was aware of his actions. I must be to blame, I reasoned. I was involved and felt dirty and ashamed. Therefore, in my mind, I was the bad one, not Walter.

June 1991 (age 15)

Why is it that one minute I am full of excitement for life, thankful to be alive, full of dreams for my future, and the next minute I'm in utter despair, feeling like a black hole is sucking me in, feeling completely hopeless, daydreaming about suicide? When will this end? Where is my hope?

Feeling intense guilt, some victims struggle with the fact that their bodies physically responded to the sexual stimulation of the abuse (not realizing this is an automatic response). Many teenagers, especially, think they should have known better or could have stopped it. There are a number of reasons victims blame themselves for the abuse:

- I didn't stop it.
- It felt good.
- I liked the attention and/or special privileges and gifts.
- I continually went back to the abuser or put myself in situations that resulted in abuse—even though I sensed it was wrong.
- I should have been smarter. I knew all along that something was wrong, but I ignored the truth.

- I should have pushed him away, "wakened," run away, screamed for help, told someone sooner.

Yet victims need to understand there's nothing they could have done, and they are in no way at fault, no matter what the abuser may have told them or how old they were at the time of the abuse. The blame always rests on the abuser's shoulders.

For me, as with most victims, it took awhile for this truth to sink in. I had to understand that at the time of the abuse, I was an innocent little child with no way to protect myself. The guilt I felt was false guilt. I forgave myself—though I didn't need forgiveness for anything—because I was in no way responsible for Walter's actions. Once I began to let go of the self-blame, a huge burden lifted.

Fear awakened

In counseling, Marie and I talked a lot about my fear of social situations. I hated the fact that I was missing

May 1991 (age 15)

Right now I'm sitting on my bed, crying my eyes out. I just had another blow-up with my parents. But I'm beginning to realize some things. There is so much rage inside me that needs to come out, and I have a short fuse. I never calmly talk through a problem with the other person. I either yell and scream or ignore the person I'm mad at while seething inside. It has become a habit for me.

out on so many normal teenage experiences. I feared going to football and basketball games at school because I couldn't handle people looking at me, let alone talking to me. I feared the frightening world outside where people could hurt me, so I hid in the safety of my room rather than risk any more pain. The fears ran deep, and I didn't know how to loosen their powerful grip.

Marie suggested that becoming more assertive might help me socially. My passive approach to life, a survival skill, left little room for excitement and joy to enter in. "Most victims need help developing their assertiveness skills," Marie assured me. We talked about the differences among nonassertive, aggressive, and assertive people and behaviors:

- Non-assertive people tend to be shy, hesitant, timid, and accommodating. They don't state their opinions, needs, and feelings. I could relate to that. I rarely talked about my feelings and needs, preferring to let people guess. Honesty required too much vulnerability.

  Nonassertive people tend to walk away in order to avoid any type of confrontation. Because they don't respect themselves, they don't feel justified standing up for their views, needs, and feelings. I saw myself in that description, too.

- Aggressive people tend to be bossy, loud, demanding, tough, and dominating. These people express their opinions, needs, and feelings regardless of how it might hurt others. They often blame other people for anything that goes wrong. Aggressive people don't respect others, only themselves.

- Assertive people, however, tend to be honest, open, and direct as they express their opinions, needs, and feelings in appropriate ways. They tend to be confident, respecting others as well as themselves.

Dealing with fear

Becoming assertive was a difficult process for me, filled with determination, setbacks, and tears of frustration. I was so used to keeping secrets that I feared revealing even surface things, let alone anything meaningful. Yet slowly I began finding my voice, feeling more comfortable talking with people, even initiating conversations. I celebrated each small victory. And the victories did come—slowly but surely.

As my self-esteem grew and I began to respect myself more, I risked opening up more. And people began to notice changes in me. They said I seemed happier and more comfortable talking with people rather than always sitting quietly and listening. And I noticed something stirring inside me that I hadn't felt in a long time—hope.

Anger awakened

But the main emotion that surfaced was anger. Unfortunately, I was angry with everyone but Walter.

I had focused my anger inward, which developed into depression and self-criticism. I had focused it on my family and friends, who became innocent targets of uncontrollable rage at times. But I couldn't focus my anger on Walter, no matter how hard I tried. I knew my parents were angry at him, yet they were also concerned about him. They wanted Walter to get counseling rather than get thrown in jail. I didn't understand their compassion. It made me even angrier and more frustrated.

As the anger began to find its proper target, I admitted I wanted him to get help, but I also I wanted him punished.

Marie helped me see this struggle from a new perspective. "He may not be judged and get his rightful punishment here on earth, but God will judge him," she said. "You may not always find much comfort in that fact—because most likely Walter never will fully understand what he did and confess to it while he's still on earth—but try to remember that God is the Ultimate Judge."

I did find comfort in knowing that the final outcome was in God's hands.

Anger rechanneled

I knew it wasn't fair to take out this anger on my parents, and I began to I look for appropriate ways to deal with it.

First, I found that writing—both poetry and journal entries—helped me diminish anger's power. I could say anything I wanted in my journals. I could be honest. There was freedom in that. I could record my feelings and keep track of my progress—and what often seemed the lack of progress.

I also started playing piano again, something I hadn't done for four years. I released a lot of anger as I pounded on the keys. Playing the same song over and over again helped me express my feelings through music. All of sudden I was playing every day—which pleased my mother, a piano teacher.

Right in my own backyard—almost by accident—I found another way to handle the emotional upheaval in my life. In my journal I wrote:

> Today I discovered a quiet place, a place so serene it's almost magical. It's a muddy creek surrounded by the most beautiful woods I've ever seen. For all my fifteen years, I've never cared about this place. I've never taken the time to explore it and see it for what it really is. As I sit here in the midst of it all, I open my eyes and ears for the first time and soak in the sights and sounds of the current gently moving along, the birds chirping, and the wind blowing.
>
> I find peace here. It's a place where I can get away from all the struggles of life and find renewed strength and, quite possibly, the will to live. Since I usually do everything in my power to stay out of the woods, this experience has been something special.
>
> Buds are popping out of the trees, a sign of spring. New beginnings. It's so nice to see everything turning green. Maybe this is a sign that the season of winter in my soul is soon over, too.

Writing, music, and spending time in nature helped me cope with many emotions during that time, and they're still great stress relievers for me today. It's important for victims to find activities that help them through the emotional upheaval of the healing process. (See suggestions at the end of this chapter.)

It took awhile before I could fully direct my anger at Walter. But as I began to realize all he had stolen, rage and grief seemed to control me. I didn't deal with the grief for some time, but I desperately fought to free myself of anger's power.

The question of confrontation

After several months of counseling, Marie began talking about whether I wanted to confront Walter. I understood that confrontation can be a powerful healing tool in several ways. Victims can

- be honest about their anger

- stop hiding

- name the wrong and bring it to the light

- let the abuser know he or she hurt them

- open the door for the abuser to express remorse and repentance. (Repentance seldom happens, but victims can find freedom and healing either way.)

Yet confrontation can also be devastating. The thought of talking to Walter face to face scared me. I wasn't ready, and I didn't know if I ever would be. I wanted him to know how much he hurt me, yet I feared even being in the same room with him. He still had power over me, and he didn't even know it. I feared sabotaging my progress if I faced him. I wasn't strong enough.

I now believe that confrontation should occur only when there is more healing than pain in a person's life. Confrontations should not be done alone, and their success should not be judged by whether the abuser apologizes or not. (Most will deny anything happened.)

Another way to confront

When Marie suggested I write Walter a letter instead of confronting him face to face, I liked the idea. I had become used to pouring out all my feelings on paper. Still, I put it off for several months. I wanted that letter to be perfect, delineating all I had been through and all I was feeling, so Walter would understand the devastation he caused in my life. I also wanted him to take responsibility for his actions. And I wanted to prevent him from ever abusing another little child.

When I finally wrote the letter, pouring out my rage and grief on paper proved empowering and therapeutic.

My parents read the letter and gently said, "Christa, there's a lot of hate in this."

I didn't even realize that. But when they brought it to my attention, I wondered whether I should send the letter. Though I intended to, I never did.

In our human nature, feelings of hatred toward someone who has done something so devastating to us are natural, but in time I had to confess these feelings before God. And now that I'm further along in the healing process, I have forgiven Walter, and I'm glad I didn't send the letter. But this is a personal choice. Every victim needs to do what seems right for him or her.

Anger—an honest emotion

As I continued to deal with anger, I learned it's an honest emotion, but the question is, What are we going to do with it? We can't bury it within.

As I read the Psalms, I saw that King David honestly expressed his anger at God often. What a relief! I needed to be honest with God about my anger, too. He hadn't stopped the abuse, and I wanted to know why.

Jesus also expressed His anger (John 2:12–16), but all of His anger was righteous. Not all of ours is. In Ephesians 4:26–27, Paul writes, "In your anger do not sin: Do not let the sun go down while you are still angry, and do not give the devil a foothold." We can't allow hatred to grow.

Activities to help victims during emotional upheaval

- journaling
- writing poetry
- writing letters
- exercising
- listening to music
- playing a musical instrument
- painting, sculpting, other types of art
- talking to a caring friend or family member
- going for a walk outdoors, enjoying nature

"The sin of sexual abuse against a child is certainly cause for intense anger," write Lynn Heitritter and Jeanette Vought. "Often the child is neither able nor allowed to express that anger, and as a result the sun 'goes down' on this anger again and again. Thus, the Devil seizes the opportunity to convert righteous anger into hate, bitterness, [and] depression."[1]

Again and again I dealt with the anger issue. It affected many of my relationships. Not knowing how to handle it appropriately, I often allowed it to fester, poisoning my friendships. Even four years after I started counseling I wrote in my journal:

My friends and I have been in a huge fight for the past few weeks, and I know a lot of it is my fault. We talked everything out, and I realized even more that because of my abuse, I can't handle conflict, tension, and anger very well. As we talked, I cried the whole time. I didn't realize how many emotions I still have walled up inside of me. My friends were very encouraging and supportive. They said maybe it was a good thing this fight happened because I can work on handling anger and conflict better now instead of facing this in marriage someday and possibly ruining that relationship.

Positive emotions awakened

But as I learned to express the negative emotions I had suppressed so long, I found I was making room for positive emotions to reawaken as well. Little by little, life seemed less of a burden. God began to show me signs of true living: I began to smile, laugh, and feel a joy I hadn't felt for a long time.

Even tears were a gift. I was becoming more comfortable with my emotions. I still had a hard time talking about my feelings, but at least I was finally feeling again. I preferred anything over the deadness I'd known for so long. Being alive means experiencing fully life's joy and sorrow, laughter and tears. The joy makes the pain more bearable, and the pain makes the joy that much sweeter.

The bud was beginning to blossom, a sweet delight to my soul. The metamorphosis came with pain, as I continued to find out, yet somehow that made the transformation even more beautiful.

May 1991 (age 15)

I think I'm slowly stepping out of my secure shell. One day my friends and I were in a silly mood. All of a sudden we were all laughing. Me, too! What a tremendous release! I couldn't even remember the last time I had laughed. All I knew were tears. We have had laugh attacks almost every day at school, and it is such a sign of hope for me. With each small victory I feel a little more free from the past. I think I'm going to make it.

With hope again within my grasp, I reached out and clung to it with everything in me. The light was beginning to pierce the darkness of my soul, and I was so thankful. Maybe God had been listening to my pleas for mercy all along. The nightmares had ceased, and the fear was lessening as I continued to expose the monster to the light.

I remember when Mom and I were looking for a Bible verse for my confirmation back in 1990, we chose Jeremiah 29:11: "'For I know the plans I have for you,' declares the LORD, 'plans to prosper you and not to harm you, plans to give you hope and a future.'" That verse became even more meaningful as I began working through the effects of my abuse.

I had lived so long without hope, believing I had no future or—if I did—that it would be bleak. Now God seemed to be saying to me, "Don't believe Satan's lies. I have wonderful things planned for you. Don't give up. Keep trusting me and following me. Your hope is in me, and I won't disappoint you."

I clung to that verse—my ray of hope. I wasn't about to let it go. Having started to climb out of the pit, these signs along the journey told me I was closer to the light.

God's promises for those who are depressed or suicidal

When you feel God couldn't possibly love you . . .

Psalm 32:10 "Many are the woes of the wicked, but the LORD's unfailing love surrounds the [person] who trusts in him."

Romans 8:38–39 "I am convinced that nothing can ever separate us from [God's] love. Death can't, and life can't. The angels won't, and all the powers of hell itself cannot keep God's love away. Our fears for today, our worries about tomorrow, or where we are—high above the sky, or in the deepest ocean—nothing will ever be able to separate us from the love of God demonstrated by our Lord Jesus Christ when he died for us" (TLB).

When you feel you can't take any more pain . . .

1 Corinthians 10:13 "God will never let you down; he'll never let you be pushed past your limit; he'll always be there to help you come through it" (The Message).

2 Corinthians 12:9 " 'My grace is sufficient for you, for my power is made perfect in weakness.' "

Job 36:15 "But those who suffer he delivers in their suffering; he speaks to them in their affliction."

Romans 8:28 "We know that in all things God works for the good of those who love him, who have been called according to his purpose."

When you feel God is far away . . .

Psalm 139:5–10 "You hem me in—behind and before; you have laid your hand upon me. Such knowledge is too wonderful for me, too lofty for me to attain. Where can I go from your Spirit? Where can I flee from your presence? If I go up to the heavens, you are there; if I make my bed in the depths, you are there. If I rise on the wings of the dawn, if I settle on the far side of the sea, even there your hand will guide me, your right hand will hold me fast."

Isaiah 43:2–4 "When you pass through the waters, I will be with you; and when you pass through the rivers, they will not sweep over you. When you walk through the fire, you will not be burned; the flames will not set you ablaze. For I am the LORD, your God, the Holy One of Israel, your Savior. . . . you are precious and honored in my sight . . . I love you."

Matthew 28:20 "Surely I am with you always, to the very end of the age."

When you can't see any hope . . .

2 Corinthians 5:7 "We live by faith, not by sight."

Romans 8:24–26 "Hope that is seen is no hope at all. Who hopes for what he already has? But if we hope for what we do not yet have, we wait for it patiently. In the same way, the Spirit helps us in our weakness. We do not know what we ought to pray for, but the Spirit himself intercedes for us with groans that words cannot express."

Psalm 126:5–6 "Those who sow in tears will reap with songs of joy. He who goes out weeping, carrying seed to sow, will return with songs of joy, carrying sheaves with him."

When you think the darkness will never end . . .

Psalm 139:11–13 "If I say, 'Surely the darkness will hide me and the light become night around me,' even the darkness will not be dark to you; the night will shine like the day, for darkness is as light to you. For you created my inmost being."

Job 12:22 "He reveals the deep things of darkness and brings deep shadows into the light."

Isaiah 42:16 "I will turn the darkness into light before them and make the rough places smooth. These are the things I will do; I will not forsake them."

When you think God doesn't care . . .

1 Peter 5:7 "Cast all your anxiety on him because he cares for you."

Nahum 1:7 "The LORD is good, a refuge in times of trouble. He cares for those who trust in him."

Isaiah 40:11 "He tends his flock like a shepherd: He gathers the lambs in his arms and carries them close to his heart."

John 1:16 "From the fullness of his grace we have all received one blessing after another."

[1]Lynn Heitritter and Jeanette Vought, *Helping Victims of Sexual Abuse* (Minneapolis: Bethany House, 1989), p. 177.

CHAPTER 6

Little Girl Lost, Little Girl Found

Please, Lord, teach us to laugh again;
but God, don't ever let us forget that we cried.[1]

Bill Wilson

One night, about a month after I started counseling, a huge spring rainstorm soaked our small Minnesota town. The next morning I went down to the river to see how far it had expanded from the heavy rainfall the night before. I had never seen the river that high and wide. When I came to a huge area where the river had overflowed into the meadow, I decided to step right into the water and walk across the flooded ground. I had never done anything like that in my fifteen years of existence! As one foot sloshed in front of the other, the muddy water reached my knees, soaking my sweatpants. I waded in again in another part of the meadow, then followed the watery paths between the bushes and trees. It was so much fun!

The next day my brother and I talked Mom into coming with us to explore the meadow on the other side of the river. Planning ahead this time to get wet, we dressed in old clothes. My brother lost no time getting waist deep in a ditch. When we got to the meadow, he plunged across, the water reaching his chest. After a while, I ventured across, sure this would be the only opportunity in my life to swim in a meadow!

> *May 1991 (age 15)*
>
> *Today we not only enjoyed being together, but we enjoyed feeling like little kids again. I felt happy and carefree. It was a wonderful, simple time. I was surprised and delighted that Mom joined us. For some reason all the memory-making things we did today gave me hope for the future. I'm so thankful.*

The child within

That summer and in the months following I allowed myself to enjoy "little kid things"—climbing trees, taking walks in the rain, playing in the sand at the beach, exploring the woods, playing on a jungle gym and swings, collecting dolls, coloring with my cousin, jumping in a pile of leaves, and going sledding. Trying to make up for lost time, I found myself doing these things I never would have done before. It felt great! And I still love doing them.

About that time I also began reading about "the child within," and an idea flashed through my mind: I wonder if, over the years, the reason I wanted so much to be treated like an adult was that I didn't want to acknowledge the vulnerability of being a child. I thought of holidays and vacations with extended family. Preferring the mature, adult world to the innocence I saw in each of the other kids, I refused to play with my cousins. And I'd often get very upset when my aunts treated me like a child rather than the adult I was trying to be.

Sometimes I wish I could go back to when I was six or seven. Back to my innocence.

A case of murder

The abuse, in effect, murdered the first-grade child I was. Gone were the days of innocence, such as the day I believed I'd found "diamonds" in the snow. In one of my clearest memories from kindergarten, my friend and I went outside at recess to an area where the snowbanks were high. The pure, white snowflakes sparkled brilliantly. Instead of playing house, we pretended we had a little store, and we would pack the snow in squares and pile them up so we could get as many of them in our store as possible. Innocence had room for fun.

Innocence also believed in a decent world where people could be trusted. Innocence was an illusion. The abuse flung me into an evil, adult world I hadn't known existed. After the abuse, I may have seemed to play like other kids, yet I can't say I fully enjoyed playing. How could

I? I felt such fear and contempt for everything related to being a child.

The vulnerability of the little girl who had been abused terrified me so much that I, myself, tried to destroy her. To prevent any more pain, I subconsciously vowed never again to be weak and needy. I had to be in control at all times. In my first-grader logic, the price of safety and control equaled disconnection from anything spontaneous, playful, and carefree—characteristics not associated with control.

As a result, I became fragmented. For years I held back: part of me still experienced normal childhood activities while another part strained to become a strong, powerful, invulnerable adult. Although this is a common feeling for children and adolescents, I think my abuse made me almost obsessive about it. Having concluded that trust wasn't safe and dependence was bad, I tried to create my own self-sufficient world.

As I faced the world with masks of control and confidence, my real self cowered in a dark corner inside, surrounded by invisible walls of protection. The desire for control resulted in perfectionism, overwhelming anxiety about the unknown, and problems with authority—including my parents.

New insights

But God was beginning to teach me some things. In the middle of one big fight with my parents one day, I realized something: Years before, someone in authority stole my trust and hurt me immeasurably. As I began to understand my reaction, I began to feel more comfortable submitting to my parents and others God had placed in authority over my life.

I started identifying my anxiety triggers: experiencing new things, meeting new people, and feeling unable to control the outcome of an event. These things still cause anxiety—to a degree. But little by little God has helped me confront them head-on. Each time I face the unknown and meet with success, I find more confidence. I can identify with the psalmist who wrote, "When anxiety was great within me, your consolation brought joy to my soul" (Psalm 94:19).

God consoled me often, reminding me of past anxiety-filled situations in which He filled me with peace and brought me through stronger, able to trust Him more. All these things have helped me let go and be more flexible.

As one who spent nearly a decade hiding, I found it very difficult to risk escaping from my comfort zone, yet again and again God has shown me that healing and growth don't happen when we are comfortable.

Little girl found

After years of being out of touch with a part of myself, it was with great thanksgiving that I began to go back and reconnect my fragmented self with the frightened child within me. It wasn't a scary process for me because I desperately wanted to integrate all I had lost.

I still wouldn't allow myself to grieve my losses. That would come later. But things like walking through puddles brought a measure of healing. Allowing myself to play and be childlike, I could embrace life with the joy of being real and whole.

Jesus had a special place in His heart for children (Mark 10:13–16). He wrapped His arms around the very children the disciples thought were being a bother. Jesus said, in effect, that the Kingdom belonged to those who were like the children He held, those who wouldn't allow anything to distort their view of the Creator and His Creation, those who maintained a sense of awe and wonder at both simple and complex things—from an autumn leaf to personal relationships (Psalm 19:1).

> *August 22, 1991 (age 15)*
>
> *I had the best time at the cabin last week, which normally is my least favorite place to go. I realized how beautiful and peaceful everything is there. It was like a veil was lifted from my eyes, and I saw things around me differently. The beauty invaded my soul. Sunsets were the best part. It was a splendid sight to watch the Master Artist paint the sky, and I thanked Him many times for His goodness.*

Those with a childlike mind-set have a sense of astonishment at all they see and experience and a keen anticipation of everything yet to come. Author and radio host Rich Buhler writes:

> Childlikeness is the quality of being delightfully real with myself, with God, and when possible, with others. . . . Childlikeness is really wholeheartedness. That's what I think of when I think of children. They trust wholeheartedly. They have fun wholeheartedly. They get angry wholeheartedly.

They hurt wholeheartedly. One of the tragic effects of victimization is to fragment that childlike wholeheartedness. The ability to trust, to feel, to have fun, and to grieve in a wholehearted way is injured. That leaves the victim in a state where he can "sort of" trust, "sort of" have fun, or, "sort of" be honest about pain.[2]

What a breakthrough it was to begin doing things I only wished I had done or things I hadn't fully experienced as a child! For example, as I was growing up, I generally avoided physical contact—including giving people hugs and sitting in my dad's lap—things I had done before the abuse began but not afterward. My dad felt hurt, but he didn't understand why I didn't cuddle with him anymore. It was a great loss for both of us. But as I began to heal, I found myself crawling onto his lap once in a while. And as for hugging people—I now love to give hugs every chance I get.

And the newly discovered child within enjoyed a renewed relationship with cousins. After years of insisting on hanging around the adults, I began creating precious memories with cousins young and old. Through having tea parties with my girl cousins, playing cards, wrestling with the guys (and my winning, of course!), getting teased, or having good talks, God has been helping me rebuild these relationships. Each memory is a priceless treasure, another reminder of my victory, and a cause for thanksgiving to the One who made it all possible.

I still enjoy doing "little kid things," and I hope I

always will. In fact, one recent Easter I took part in not one, but two Easter egg hunts! One was a group event, but the other was just for me. I almost demanded that my parents hide eggs for me—as they had every other year—even though my brother wouldn't be home to hunt them with me. My parents obliged, and Dad said he had fun finding unique places to hide them.

My friends thought having an Easter egg hunt at my age was strange, but not when you consider that my childlike excitement about it is, for me, a definite sign of progress. I quit trying to grow up so fast and began enjoying "being in the moment."

It's not so much the childlike experiences themselves as it is a childlike mind-set that has transformed the way I'm learning to view life. The ordinary has become spectacular. The common has become a peek into heaven.

The healing in Creation

Another healing thing for me has been spending time outside in nature. It's helped me switch focus from my pain to the captivating beauty all around me that I'd been blind to before. I began taking walks outside and finding a peace I'd never felt before.

God opened my eyes to the details in life, and I haven't closed them since. I started to see that regardless of how it may seem, God is not silent. Nature shouts His presence and power. "Since the creation of the world," Paul writes, "God's invisible qualities—his eternal power and divine nature—have been clearly seen, being understood from what has been made, so that men are without excuse"

(Romans 1:20).

God was speaking to me through all He created. I marveled at deep blue skies, fresh country air, the peacefulness of a wilderness lake, the gentle flowing of a stream, the pounding of ocean waves, and the tranquility of gazing at the stars. I could certainly trust the all-powerful Creator of the universe to restore my life and heal my wounded soul. God renewed my strength as I continued to put my hope in Him (Isaiah 40:25–31). Glimpses of His power in Creation reassured me He wasn't about to let me fall.

A sense of awe

I remember when I was a young girl, being filled with awe every Christmas after we decorated the tree and turned on the lights. It was such a beautiful sight that my brother and I started a tradition of sleeping in front of the tree, staring at those fabulous lights until our dreary eyes closed for a night's sleep. Years later, that awe has returned—along with the temptation to sleep in front of the Christmas tree.

Being childlike is a gift from God, and I will never cease to thank Him for it. As I brought that frightened child into the light, my sense of wonder and excitement returned. Perfectionism stopped controlling me. Being the best no longer defined my self-esteem. Rather, doing my personal best became my goal and gave me satisfaction.

Gazing at the dazzling spectacle of the setting sun or city lights dancing in the night brings peace and strength to my soul. Why? Because I'm winning the battle over the need for control. Life is no longer filled with fears and doubts but rather with hope for an exciting future. Trust is possible as we open ourselves to the One who can do the impossible—teaching us to laugh again, to find healing from past emotional wounds, and maybe even to discover diamonds in the snow.

> *Praise the Lord, O my soul;*
>   *all my inmost being, praise his holy name.*
> *Praise the Lord, O my soul,*
>   *and forget not all his benefits—*
> *who forgives all your sins*
>   *and heals all your diseases,*
> *who redeems your life from the pit*
>   *and crowns you with love and compassion,*
> *who satisfies your desires with good things*
>   *so that your youth is renewed like the eagle's.*
>   *Psalm 103:1–5*

[1]Bill Wilson in *Thoughts for My Secret Pal: 101 Thoughts for You,* Paul C. Brownlow, ed. (Ft. Worth: Brownlow Publishing Company, 1994) #92.

[2]Rich Buhler, *Pain and Pretending* (Nashville: Thomas Nelson, 1991), pp. 148–149.

CHAPTER 7

Stepping from the Shadows

For there is nothing hidden that will not be disclosed,
and nothing concealed that will not be known
or brought out into the open.

Luke 8:17

August 16, 1991 (age 15)

    It's a quarter to one, and I can't get to sleep. I'm thinking about how I will tell my relatives about my abuse. I keep thinking of all the missed opportunities to get to know them. I feel so guilty, angry, and sad for acting the way I did. The grief is overwhelming. Tears are making rivers down my cheeks.

I've been going through pictures and have run across several of me when I was very young. I'm surprised at how little and innocent I was when the abuse started. I can't understand how anyone could violate a child.

Mourning my losses

When I first read that victims must go through a grieving process, I was confused. Why did I have to grieve? Eventually I began to see many losses I needed to mourn, yet the timing had to be right for my mind to deal with each one.

My grieving process began when I realized I'm not the same person I was before the abuse. A part of me died, and I could never regain it, so I needed to mourn. Questions of "what might have been" tortured my mind over and over.

Perhaps most of all I grieved my lost innocence. Often, watching little children the age I was at the time of the abuse triggered intense grief. Seeing their innocence and exuberance reminded me of what Walter stole from me.

But I also had to grieve my lost self-worth, lost joy, lost time and opportunities. Trying to restore the damage the abuse caused took a great deal of time and effort. And then there were the lost relationships—I mourned relationships full of problems and relationships that never had a chance to develop. I grieved my distorted view of God and my shattered trust in myself, in people, in the world, and in my heavenly Father.

And I mourned my lost feelings of safety. I don't remember a time I felt safe. The abuse destroyed my belief in the goodness of people. Unfortunately grieving isn't a one-

December 6, 1991 (age 15)

Our bus driver got us stuck in the snow today, so a man picked us up in the school's station wagon. The whole way home I was so scared. I knew that after this man dropped off my friend, I would be alone with him. I was afraid he might rape me—though I had no cause for my fear. I blame it on the abuse and my total lack of trust. Why must I live like this? I can't experience true freedom because I'm always afraid something could happen. Should I be thankful for this fear so I never become careless? Or should I be enraged that what was stolen affects how I look at everything around me?

time event; new issues arise and old ones resurface. Grief can't be ignored or denied because if we don't process it, it's a slow-acting poison that grows more deadly later in life.

Letting go

My losses ran deep, and it wasn't easy to let them go. As I grieved, I felt a deep sadness and cried a lot. Sometimes it seemed God ignored my pleas for mercy.

The psalmist Asaph said he cried out to the Lord when he was in distress, yet his soul "refused to be comforted." "I thought about the former days, the years of long ago. . . . Will the LORD reject forever?" he asked. "Has his unfailing love vanished . . . for all time?" (Psalm 77:2–8). Then Asaph recalls the miracles God performed while leading His

Summer 1991 (age 15)

I just got back from youth group at church. I sat quietly most of the evening just staring. My eyes welled up with tears, and I'd wipe them away. Often I hold back the tears so no one will see them, but tonight I wanted people to see them, to see my pain. I don't think anyone noticed. No one said a word. After a year of such intense withdrawal and change, you would think someone would take the time to figure out why this is happening. It seems no one cares. Tonight I wanted to tell everyone about the abuse. After keeping it a secret so long, I feel like screaming it until people listen. When no one responded to my tears and my silence tonight, I grew more and more depressed. And I had thought I was getting better!

people from despair to victory, and he counts on God to do it again.

That's what I had to do, too. As I've grieved, God has reminded me of all the miracles He's performed so far, and He isn't finished yet. Because He's proven Himself faithful, I have no reason to think He will ever let me down.

The Bible says there's a time for everything: "a time to weep and a time to laugh, a time to mourn and a time to dance" (Ecclesiastes 3:4). Each season of grief passes, and I come through stronger and freer because I faced it with God's help.

Stepping stones to joy

As I allowed myself to mourn the losses that kept me from moving on, I began to accept them and let them go. The abuse stole much, but it didn't destroy me. I survived, and my seasons of grief, though difficult, became stepping stones to joy and to the full life God intended.

Amid all the painful memories, I also had many happy ones. And I began to realize that if I didn't go back and embrace them, Walter would continue to have power over me. I couldn't change my past, but I could control my attitude toward it and toward the future.

A couple of years ago, I wrote in my journal:

> Every so often God gives me a memory that leaves me smiling, sometimes laughing, and always filled with joy. Now when I look through my photo albums, I don't see pain reflected but cherished moments of laughter and fun with family and friends.

Secret shadows

During that summer after I told my parents about the abuse, I made a difficult decision. Hoping for a fresh start, I decided to transfer to another high school in the fall for my sophomore year. Unrealistically, despite emotional setbacks during the authorities' ongoing investigation, I expected my healing work to be done before the first day of school arrived.

Already fearful of the inevitable changes—stepping out of my comfortable surroundings, trying to find my way around a new campus, and making new friends—I didn't need a heavy sadness hanging over my head. I needed some measure of success.

Though healing had begun, the secrecy about my abuse was still choking me. Only a few people knew what I was going through. I was afraid to tell others about my weekly counseling sessions and my daily emotional battles.

I had to be two different people—to those who knew my secret I could be honest about my struggles and my victories; to those who didn't I had to pretend everything was fine. I began to feel trapped, concealing the very thing that, to a great extent, shaped who I am.

I was sick of hiding yet scared to come out of the shadows—my safety and comfort. I wanted to reach out. But how? Though desperate for people to care about me, I was scared I'd only confirm my worst fear—that I wasn't worth caring about.

My silence was a cry for help, yet no one seemed to be listening. Had I become so good at acting and staying in control that no one knew about my private hell?

Going public

A passion was stirring within me to help other victims and to increase public awareness of the prevalence and devastation of sexual abuse. But as much as I wanted the secret out, the thought of actually telling people face to face drenched me with fear. I felt too fragile to risk people's reactions. The shame was still so entrenched that I wondered if I ever would be free. I soon realized that just as healing is a process, so is going public—and I felt disappointed.

June 21, 1992 (age 16)

I just got done telling my grandparents that I was abused. This was the second hardest thing I've ever done, next to telling my parents. It's strange how I can be brave at times and think I can tell the world my secret, but when the time comes, feelings of shame, embarrassment, and fear make it nearly impossible. I must be living in a dream world thinking I ever could publish my story. I hope one day I can say out loud—without looking down or flinching—that I was sexually abused. Hopefully it will get easier.

If I can't say it, I can write it, I decided, preferring to stay safe in my home and write about the truth of my painful past rather than be embarrassed by people's reactions. I feared no one would believe me—or worse, that I would feel the shame all over again. I needed the secret to come out because keeping it hidden was stifling. But even in telling my secret, safety remained my goal.

So I began writing my story, still hoping it would be published someday in our local newspaper. I would eventually realize the importance of verbalizing the secret face to face, eye to eye, individual to individual. But first I needed to take tiny steps toward that goal.

It wasn't until the following summer that I mustered the courage to tell someone besides my parents and the authorities what had happened. One weekend Mom and Dad and I invited my grandparents on my mom's side to come down for visit. There was no way I could tell them myself about the abuse, as much as I wanted to, so Dad promised to read them my written account.

As we sat in our living room, Mom began by saying, "This is going to be really hard for Christa to talk about."

Filled with shame, I started crying before Dad even started reading.

It became utter torture to hear my own story being read and to visualize the abuse happening all over again. I felt embarrassed and humiliated. *How can I still feel dirty after months of counseling?* I thought.

As Grandma listened, tears streamed down her face. Both she and Grandpa were terribly upset but supportive and caring, which was exactly what I needed. They asked questions, and to my surprise I was able to answer them.

"This explains a lot," Grandpa said.

Grandma gave me a big hug. "Looking back, now that we know the truth, I guess I can think of a number of things that might have been signs of abuse, but we had no idea."

After my grandparents learned the truth, I knew I had to tell all my aunts, uncles, and cousins on my mom's side soon. Again I decided to take the easy way out. From the safety of my home I wrote each of them a letter and enclosed a copy of my story. That way I didn't have to face them or say the words out loud or feel the shame again as they reacted.

Safety net

About a month after I sent the letters, we vacationed at the family cabin with all the relatives I had just contacted.

Mom and Dad had been gently urging me to tell my brother, by then fourteen, because they didn't want him finding out from one of the others there. I knew I should have told him long before, but the shame stopped me. Now it was time, but again I chickened out of telling the story myself and asked Mom to explain it.

She took advantage of our travel time in the car on the way. "I have something important to tell you," she said to my brother. "Have you noticed any changes in Christa during the last year—maybe her being a little more playful in her teasing or coming out of her shell more?"

"Yeah," he replied.

Mom reminded him of all the trips to see Marie, then told him why I had to get counseling. Tears flooded my eyes as I again relived the memories.

My brother didn't react much.

"What are you thinking?" Mom asked him.

"It's a shock," he admitted, but he didn't say anything to me.

August 1, 1992 (age 16)

It feels good to finally pursue a relationship with my cousins. When I left, I even got a kiss on the cheek and a big hug from one of them. My aunt has said a few times on this trip that she can see I've changed. by my free spirit. I'm not as closed and in need of control as I used to be. On the way home, my brother, three of my girl cousins, and I had fun singing songs together, something I'd never have done before. Thank you, God, for the changes taking place.

I didn't say anything to him, either. I couldn't through all my tears. I felt guilty and sad that I didn't have the courage to tell him myself, but the shame and humiliation were worse. *How am I ever going to bring myself to say out loud that I was sexually abused?* I wondered.

During our time at the cabin all my relatives expressed their concern for me. It especially meant a lot when two of my uncles told me they really cared about me. One wrote a letter, saying he knew the abuse had caused me a lot of shame, but he wanted me to know how much they all loved me and would be praying for me.

I was so relieved! I no longer had to hide my secret from them. I was beginning to feel something new—freedom.

One night, cousin Jerry and I took the canoe out and had a wonderful time talking and getting to know each other better. He mentioned that he and his brother Dave had wondered what I'd be like this time because in the past I'd been moody when our families got together. They remembered times when I'd fight with Mom and stay away from everyone.

I felt sad and angry that the effects of my abuse had basically ruined my relationship with my cousins—even though neither they nor I, at the time, fully realized what was happening.

Dave and Jerry obviously saw a change in me while we were together because they started teasing me. I laughed and played along with it. Two years earlier I wouldn't have felt free to laugh and joke like that. For the rest of our vacation I became the target of their teasing, pillow fights, wrestling matches, and tickling contests. I just didn't think it was fair that they were so strong, and I couldn't do anything to get them back!

I was happy to see that safety net of supportive people coming around me, as Wanda had advised, but I wasn't doing well at verbalizing what had happened to me. I knew that was my next step—a step that took almost another year.

Saying the words

The next spring, when I was seventeen, we made a special trip to see my grandma (Dad's widowed mother) so that we could tell her, my aunt, uncle, and cousins about the abuse. Grandma's fiance, Morrie, to whom she's now married, would also be there. During the three hours in the car, I fought within myself. I was determined to tell my secret myself this time. I didn't want to—because I was afraid of everyone's reactions—but I knew I had to. This was the sole purpose of the trip.

But throughout the day, I stalled. We ate, watched TV, and played games while I tried to build up my courage. Finally, when we were all gathered in the living room, I sat down next to Grandma and Morrie on the couch and said, "There's something I need to tell all of you." As I started talking, I was surprised to find myself very much in control. I didn't even cry. "It's something that has affected my life in many ways, but I want you to know I'm going to be okay."

I took a deep breath and then said the awful words straight out: "In first grade I was sexually abused by Walter."

My relatives sat there in shock. Tears came, especially from Grandma. Then Dad, Mom, and I answered questions about everything—from whether we were going to court to various ways it has affected my self-image and behavior.

I didn't know what my grandmother would do when she learned about the abuse. Though devastated, she chose not to hide our family's heartache. She shared with many in our extended family the article I hoped would be published in the newspaper. They responded with concern and support, and I was very grateful!

I realized I truly was worthy of love and care. My entire family's support and willingness to talk about such a secretive issue has, without a doubt, been a major force in helping me become whole.

Being able to verbalize what happened was a huge accomplishment. It gave me hope. The more I brought my secret out into the light, the less power it had over me. Each time I told my secret, I took giant steps forward. And as I continued to say the words, the precious light of truth swallowed up the darkness of my soul.

Opening eyes

Something good was already coming out of my pain. By simply telling my story—even to my relatives—I was educating people. Several family members said they appreciated the advice to talk with their kids about these matters and promptly did so. An issue that had once been easy to ignore now hit close to home. None of us could deny its reality any longer.

As the news spread among my family, three people came to me and said they had been abused as well. At first I was shocked. Then I realized that I, too, was buying into the myth that abuse doesn't happen to "nice Christian people." No family is immune.

Abuse is rampant, yet only a fraction of abuse victims come forward. And when one person braves the light of exposure, it gives others courage to talk about their pain.

In the past six years, I have had many opportunities to tell my story, and usually at least one person comes to me afterward to tell me that he or she was also abused. Fear can imprison us when we feel we're alone in the dark, but coming together in the light brings strength and freedom.

As more and more people found out about my abuse, I was shocked at their compassionate reaction. I would cry every time, deeply touched by the realization that people cared about me and wanted to know how I was doing. For more than eight years I had believed Satan's lie that I wasn't worth caring about. I believed I was garbage, not even worthy to live. The abuse had engraved the word *worthless* on my soul, and I had to fight those feelings constantly.

But as I began to see that I mattered to people and that they loved me for who I am, I started to accept myself. And each caring word massaged a healing balm into my fragile self-esteem.

Compassion for others

My passion to help other people only grew as God instilled in me a deep compassion for others. I was beginning to focus outward. My own pain had taught me that the fundamental need of all of us, as human beings, is to know someone loves and cares for us. I wanted to be the one to reach out to those desperate for this kind of caring, just as people were reaching out to me. Hating the thought of wasted pain, I had to pass along what God was teaching me. And as I accepted other people's love for me, I had more to give. Jesus put it this way: "'Love your neighbor as yourself'" (Mark 12:31).

I'm learning that godly service is an outpouring of love and compassion from a heart filled with love for God, others, and ourselves. Service rendered in order to fill the emptiness within or to avoid facing our own pain is neither authentic nor motivated by love.

In their book *Helping Victims of Sexual Abuse,* Lynn Heitritter and Jeanette Vought write:

> The degree to which people are convinced that they are loved unconditionally; that they are valuable, gifted and special; and that they are not alone to face life's struggles is the same degree to which they will be able to love, serve and build others up. The degree to which individuals are not convinced of these things is the same degree to which they will function out of emptiness and shame."[1]

I was grateful for the growth that had been taking place, but the journey wasn't close to being over. I still had more to learn about how to love myself and how to deal with the effects of abuse in my own life.

Promises from God for those who are grieving

When you think your grief is going to swallow you . . .

Lamentations 3:21–23, 32 "This I call to mind and therefore I have hope: Because of the LORD's great love we are not consumed, for his compassions never fail. They are new every morning; great is your faithfulness. . . . Though he brings grief, he will show compassion, so great is his unfailing love. For he does not willingly bring affliction or grief."

When you think no one understands your grief . . .

Isaiah 53:4 "He is . . . acquainted with grief. . . . Surely he has borne our griefs and carried our sorrows" (NKJV).

Psalm 10:14 "But you, O God, do see trouble and grief; you consider it to take it in hand. The victim commits himself to you; you are the helper."

When you think God doesn't care . . .

1 Peter 5:7 "Cast all your anxiety on him because he cares for you."

Nahum 1:7 "The Lord is good, a refuge in times of trouble. He cares for those who trust in him."

Isaiah 40:11 "He tends his flock like a shepherd: He gathers the lambs in his arms and carries them close to his heart."

Psalm 139:1–3, 7, 17–18 "O Lord, you . . . know everything about me. You know when I sit or stand. When far away you know my every thought. You chart the path ahead of me, and tell me where to stop and rest. Every moment you know where I am. . . . I can never get away from my God! . . . How precious it is, Lord, to realize that you are thinking about me constantly! I can't even count how many times a day your thoughts turn towards me. And when I waken in the morning, you are still thinking of me!" (TLB).

When you think you're not worth caring about . . .

1 John 3:1 "How great is the love the Father has lavished on us, that we should be called children of God! And that is what we are!"

Luke 12:6–7 " 'Are not five sparrows sold for two pennies? Yet not one of them is forgotten by God. Indeed, the very hairs of your head are all numbered. Don't be afraid; you are worth more than many sparrows.' "

When you wonder if the pain and grief will ever end . . . .

Psalm 71:20–21 "Though you have made me see troubles, many and bitter, you will restore my life again; from the depths of the earth you will again bring me up. You will increase my honor and comfort me once again."

1 Peter 5:10 "And the God of all grace, who called you to his eternal glory in Christ . . . will himself restore you and make you strong, firm and steadfast."

Psalm 31:9, 14 "Be merciful to me, O LORD, for I am in distress; my eyes grow weak with sorrow, my soul and my body with grief . . . But I trust in you, O LORD; I say, 'You are my God.' My times are in your hands."

Psalm 30:5 "Weeping may remain for a night, but rejoicing comes in the morning."

[1]Heitritter and Vought, *Helping Victims of Sexual Abuse*, p. 66.

CHAPTER 8

Courage Meets Confidence

Being confident of this,
that he who began a good work in you
will carry it on to completion.

Philippians 1:6

I love the way God works. When I began to think more and more about helping other people and creating something positive out of all the junk I'd been through, God not only gave me opportunities but the courage to take advantage of them.

My desire for God to use me overruled my desire to be safe. I knew that meant taking risks, but I feared not making a difference more than I feared the unknown. My new school provided me with numerous occasions to help others and, in the process, help myself.

Opportunity knocks

Albert Einstein once said, "In the middle of difficulty lies opportunity." For me, my greatest opportunity was something called Project Trust. A group of high-school students visited elementary schools to perform a play called "TOUCH" created by the Illusion Theater of Minneapolis. Identifying the difference between good, bad, and confusing touch, the play aims to help kids avoid being sexually abused.

What a great opportunity! Not only was I able to give kids the message I'd always wished I could have heard when I was growing up, but I was surrounded by fellow actors who encouraged and cared about me.

I began to learn how to trust and reach out. My peers here knew the fragility of trust, and sacrificed time and energy to give kids the message of prevention so no one could take that trust away.

On the second day of workshop training for Project Trust, I pulled the leaders aside and asked them if they thought I should tell everyone that I'd been abused. With caring smiles they encouraged me to do it. Each day, before we left the workshop, we had a little discussion, and they said that would be a good opportunity to tell everyone. I agreed. But when that time came, I chickened out. I came close to speaking up, but shame and fear again washed over me.

I talked to one of the leaders afterward, and she said she would arrange another meeting with everyone if I still wanted to tell them. I did, but as the time approached, I began to get nervous again. Could I really do this?

As my directors and fellow actors sat there looking at me, I finally summoned all my courage and spoke up. "If I don't say tonight what I need to say, I'll be very disappointed with myself," I began. "I have to warn you—this is going to be tough for me to say. It's the first time I've told anyone my age . . . but . . . I, myself, was sexually abused as a child."

Everyone sat in stunned silence, and I began to see tears in a few eyes as I gave some details. Then I told them some of the ways the experience still affected me. "But doing this play has given me a lot of hope," I continued. "I'm happy to be part of the group because I know that through this I'm going to make a difference." My own

February 11, 1993 (age 17)

I'm proud of myself! I actually told my secret—and survived! It wasn't that bad. And now that I've said it, I know shame doesn't have such a powerful hold over me. I have a lot of hope. I can't explain how wonderful it feels to finally have a group of people at school who know what I'm dealing with and to know they will be there for me. I've been waiting so long to be able to walk through the halls and not feel alone. I'm excited that we're going to be helping kids so that they won't have to go through what I did. It's been an incredible and memorable two days!

tears began to flow as I thanked them for listening, and by the time I sat down I think almost everyone was crying.

Hope answers

I couldn't believe their response. Two of the guys thanked me for my honesty. "I can see what a strong person you are," one said.

What? I thought.

Then one of the girls spoke up. "I know abuse can cause poor self-esteem," she said, "but I want you to know that I think you're a beautiful person all around."

Me?

"I never would have guessed you were a victim," another girl said. "I just thought you were shy."

Several people offered to listen whenever I needed someone to talk to.

Wow!

Then another girl told us she was also an abuse victim, and suddenly I felt such great relief, knowing I wasn't alone. After the meeting broke up, I got more hugs at once than I've ever received! Many people I hardly knew told me they really cared.

My confidence grew by gigantic leaps while I performed with Project Trust. I watched in amazement as God miraculously transformed me. I knew I still had a long way to go, but I was deeply grateful for the progress God had already given. And He encouraged me in many ways—including this portion of a letter my aunt wrote to me:

When you do the play, imagine that your parents, brother, friends, and all your extended family are there giving you a standing ovation. We are all there applauding your courage. We are clapping and smiling, and we have tears running down our faces because we are proud—proud that our Christa has taken back a piece of herself by sharing the play with some kids who really need to know. It's a giant step away from victim and toward survivor.

In black and white

Having surrounded myself with a safety net of supportive people, I sensed it was time to publish my story in the newspaper. I had a strong desire to educate the community and break the silence surrounding sexual abuse. I gave the newspaper my story and waited to hear when it would be published.

Several months later, in April of 1993, I got home from school and found a phone message: the newspaper wanted to print my story the next day. When I returned the call, a woman told me they had made an editorial decision to print the article anonymously. My heart broke. All along I had thought my name would be with my story. I didn't want to hide any longer, nor did I want to give the impression that I needed to.

As the week progressed and people found out I was the one who wrote the article, I received none of the anticipated negative reactions. Kids and adults alike were sympathetic and kind. One mother called me, saying Walter had also baby-sat for her children. She thanked me profusely for

---

April 19, 1993 (age 17)

My story is finally in the newspaper! My life, my pain, my joy for all to see. All my life I'd fought to be invisible, and now I was baring my soul. I told some friends at school and in the youth group that there was an article in the newspaper I wanted them to read. That took a lot of courage for me. I'm amazed at how strong I am. The more I tell people, the easier it gets.

---

telling my story and encouraging parents to talk with their kids about abuse.

I had waited a long time for the article to appear, but that one call made it all worthwhile. And seeing my story in black and white helped me take back a little more of the power stolen from me. I truly began feeling more like a survivor than a victim.

But since my name hadn't appeared with my story, I didn't feel complete. I wanted desperately to do something more in the fight against this terrible evil.

Fighting for my voice

In God's perfect timing, shortly after I graduated from high school, I received my first opportunity to speak about my abuse to a group of one hundred teenagers. But my phobia of public speaking and my desire to be invisible did not magically disappear as I'd hoped they would.

When the time came to give my speech, I wondered what I had gotten myself into. Speeches had been the most dreaded part of school for me, and now, willingly, I'd agreed to stand in front of a roomful of high-schoolers to tell my most personal story. I was petrified of being the focus of attention with dozens of pairs of eyes looking at me and picking me apart.

What had I been thinking? Only a few years before, I couldn't even read out loud for a class of thirty because I was too self-conscious. How could I have made myself believe that things had changed so drastically in such a short amount of time?

Once I got up there, I was surprisingly calm, and the kids actually listened to what I had to say, but I wondered why God hadn't healed this part of me. Then I realized I hadn't let Him. I no longer believed I was worthless and needed to "blend in," yet the fear was automatic. It couldn't be controlled as long as I kept it in the dark, away from God's touch.

As I was reading my Bible one day, I noticed Jeremiah's response when God called him to be His messenger. "Ah, Sovereign LORD," Jeremiah said, "I do not know how to speak; I am only a child" (Jeremiah 1:6).

That was pretty much my response to God as well.

But God replied, "Do not say, 'I am only a child.' You must go to everyone I send you to and say whatever I command you. Do not be afraid of them, for I am with you and will rescue you" (vv. 7–8).

Too often we resist God's call for our lives and question whether we can be of any use to Him. Satan loves doubt and passivity.

My fear had silenced me long enough. I resolved to fight for my voice because I knew my message needed to be heard. I was terrified of becoming more vulnerable and fac-

ing the unknown. Yet, once
again, taking the risk
enabled further growth.

Eleanor Roosevelt
once said that we gain
strength, courage, and confidence when we look fear
in the face. We can say, "I
lived through this horror
and I can take the next
thing that comes along."
We must do the thing we
think we cannot do.

> I waited patiently for the LORD; he turned to me and heard my cry. He lifted me out of the slimy pit, out of the mud and mire; he set my feet on a rock and gave me a firm place to stand. He put a new song in my mouth, a hymn of praise to our God. Many will see and fear and put their trust in the LORD.
>
> PSALM 40:1–3

Sacrifice of fear

I still tend to keep
my fear of public speaking in the dark sometimes. As late as
the fall of 1997 I wrote this in my journal:

> How I wish I was like those who speak effortlessly
> and often in front of others. They seem so confi-
> dent. What is a simple, nonthreatening task to
> them utterly terrifies me. One good thing is that
> when I do speak, it requires absolute dependence
> on God. As Jesus says, "Apart from me you can do
> nothing" (John 15:5). Maybe I should be thankful
> for this area in my life where reliance on God is
> essential.

God is showing me that offering this fear to Him is
a worthy and acceptable sacrifice. His power and glory are

not revealed through human strength but through human weakness.

Paul wrote these honest words: "I came to you in weakness and fear, and with much trembling. My message and my preaching were not with wise and persuasive words, but with a demonstration of the Spirit's power, so that your faith might not rest on men's wisdom, but on God's power" (1 Corinthians 2:3–5). That's a great encouragement to me.

Speaking publicly about my experiences is important to me for two reasons:

1. Fear binds us only as much as we let it. God continues to supply me with the courage and the determination to fight, and He promises the same for anyone else.

2. It is amazing what God will do when we give ourselves to Him for His purpose. God "is able to do immeasurably more than all we ask or imagine, according to his power that is at work within us" (Ephesians 3:20). Had I relied on my own strength, I could not have said two words, let alone given a ten-minute speech. It took a miracle from God to find my voice.

Freedom to be me

As I continued to bring the truth into the light, a burden lifted from my shoulders. I walked the halls at school, free to be myself. I slowly opened up and began to show people the real Christa. My deadness transformed into a joy for living—hearty laughter, bright eyes, and smiles from the heart.

As I grew more confident, I began accepting myself with all my quirks and faults, no longer consumed by feelings of inferiority, fear of rejection, and concern over what others thought about me. I began to tear down the walls that protected yet held me captive for years. It was a slow process, but each brick laid aside created an open space where I could reach out and connect with other human beings.

One day I came upon Psalm 40:1–3, and as I read it, my eyes started getting misty. Every word, though written thousands of years before, described God's amazing work in my own life. I recalled that early image in my mind—falling into a deep, dark pit, hoping I would soon hit bottom and start climbing toward the light. It had been a long climb with many slips backward into the pit, but each step closer to the light brought more of the healing, hope, and joy I had dreamed would someday come.

I no longer blamed God for the abuse or for not stopping it. I still wondered why it happened to me, but I was not angry at Him. I forgave God—not because He needed it but because I needed to knock down the barrier in my relationship with Him.

Though at times I thought God had abandoned me, I now saw that He'd been with me every step of the journey. Sometimes He chose to be silent, but He was still right by my side giving me strength.

Drawing closer to Him

My relationship with God grew immensely. I began to realize the importance of prayer and reading the Bible because I wanted to grow closer to Him. I especially enjoyed reading the Psalms. I could relate to much of what the psalmists wrote. Their refreshing honesty about their feelings and struggles encouraged me.

I was truly learning to trust again. God had brought me out of the long, cold winter of my soul and warmed me with His penetrating light of hope. I was deeply grateful. For all the help I received from books, from my counselor, and from family and friends, I knew that true healing ultimately comes from God. He had proven faithful.

I didn't take for granted any of the work He had done in my life or the many gifts He had blessed me with—from my family's love and support to the joy of watching a beautiful sunset. I well remembered where I had been and how God had snatched me from the bottom of the pit and was redeeming my life.

Promises for those who need to build their confidence in God

Isaiah 43:4–5 "You are precious and honored in my sight, and . . . I love you . . . Do not be afraid, for I am with you."

Proverbs 3:25–26 "Have no fear of sudden disaster or of the ruin that overtakes the wicked, for the LORD will be your confidence."

2 Timothy 1:7 "God has not given us a spirit of fear, but of power and of love and of a sound mind" (NKJV).

Hebrews 4:16 "Let us then approach the throne of grace with confidence, so that we may receive mercy and find grace to help us in our time of need."

For more information about the play
entitled "TOUCH," please contact
Illusion Theater,
Sexual Abuse Prevention Program
528 Hennepin Ave, Suite 704
Minneapolis, MN 55403
(612) 339-4944

CHAPTER **9**

Longing for Closeness

You, O LORD, keep my lamp burning;
my God turns my darkness into light.
With your help I can advance against a troop
[or run through a barricade];
with my God I can scale a wall."

Psalm 18:28–29
(bracketed text mine)

As progress became more evident, I became even
more frustrated when I'd slip into old protective habits. Just
when I thought I was free, painful issues from the past came
back to haunt me. Sometimes it seemed I was taking only
one step forward and five steps back.

Many times I became frustrated and wanted to give up. Why continue fighting so hard when each victory preceded a frustrating defeat?

Relearning trust

In my impatience, I had hoped telling my secret would immediately strengthen my relationships with family and friends. After alienating myself so long, I longed to grow closer to everyone. I didn't have many friends, and the relationships I had were rather shallow. I felt no one really knew me.

I desperately wanted to be close to people, but the risk of rejection often made me shrink back. Even as I became more active socially and God blessed me with closer friendships, my need for safety short-circuited my desire for closeness. I trusted only to a degree.

I found out this wasn't unusual. According to the U.S. Department of Health and Human Services, girls sexually abused before age eighteen

> *August 11, 1994 (age 18)*
>
> *I feel so depressed. I haven't cried this much in a long time. The old thoughts of despair and hopelessness are back. I thought I had dealt with everything, but every once in a while my past knocks me for a loop, and I realize there are many issues yet to be resolved, and that hurts. It isn't fair.*
>
> *I wonder what kind of person I'd be today if I hadn't been abused. I keep thinking about all the years I lost building walls instead of bridges. There's so much I wish I could change. I wonder if I've forgiven Walter or if I ever will . . . .*

"exhibit lower levels of interpersonal function and social adjustment as adults and are less likely to form trusting relationships."

How do you learn to trust again after betrayal? Is it even possible? I clung to the hope that I could relearn what had been instinctive so long ago. I determined not to give my abuser the ultimate victory, but I knew I had a fight on my hands. In some ways I was still a prisoner of my memories.

Weak chains, strong power

Memories held me captive for at least two reasons:

1. Broken trust. Even when I was surrounded by people I felt safe with, my first-grader recollections of betrayal triggered an automatic response—erecting walls to make sure no one hurt me again.

2. Satan's lies. I believed the messages the abuse gave me—that I was not important or worth getting to know. As a child I wasn't strong enough to fight against those lies, and even as I grew older I still struggled to discern which messages were true and which came from the Enemy. At times I believed rejection was inevitable.

Why risk more pain when the odds were against me? Yet I was tired of old habits and beliefs that chained me to the past, and I desperately wanted to be free.

Josh McDowell illustrates this well in his book *His Image, My Image*:

> We're like a circus elephant tied down by a bicycle chain. We ask how one small chain could hold a powerful elephant. The trainer explains that the chain doesn't hold him; it's the elephant's memory that keeps him from trying to escape. When the elephant was very young, he didn't have the strength to break the chain or pull free. He learned then that the chain was stronger than he was and he hasn't forgotten that. The result is that the elephant, now full-grown and powerful, remembers only that he tried to break the chain and couldn't. So he never tries again. His memory, not the chain, binds him. Of course, occasionally an elephant does discover he can break the chain and from then on his keeper has trouble controlling him.[1]

Learning to trust as an adult is an extremely difficult task. As a child my trust was instinctive, but restoring stolen trust would require much time and effort. The process was slow and frustrating because my self-protection habits were so ingrained. More than a decade of not trusting can't easily be reversed.

Still needing control

Because my efforts to relearn trust and build close relationships didn't meet with instant success, I was tempted to give up. Yet I knew there was more to life, and I was determined to find out what it was. I was scared to change because I knew it would be painful, but I couldn't imagine staying the same.

Part of me wanted to completely tear down the wall that blocked my emotional connection with others, yet part of me feared losing my protection. I hoped somehow I could have the best of both worlds—safety and emotional closeness.

The part of my wall that I left standing allowed me to have control in relationships. I could jump over my wall and reach out—and even meet others' needs—when I wanted to, but the moment someone took away my control and tried to "get to me" without my permission, I retreated again behind a more impenetrable wall. I couldn't completely erase the message abuse taught me—that vulnerability only meant further hurt.

I was always the one who helped other people, but I wouldn't let anyone help me. I wore masks of independence, strength, and control, concealing my own needs. Asking for help was inconceivable—a sign of weakness. I struggled between the desire to be real and the fear of rejection. Though many people are afraid of emotional intimacy, that fear is multiplied many times over for an abuse survivor.

Male friends

Because my abuser was a man, I had cut myself off from relationships with half the population, somehow fearing every male would hurt me. It wasn't until after I told my parents about what happened that I even began talking to guys.

Though people never understood why, I rarely dated in high school. It wasn't that I didn't want to date, but fear pulled me back every time I came close. I was jealous of friends who could talk easily to guys. I literally didn't know how. Feeling uncomfortable around them, I avoided them, which they perceived as being stuck-up. If a guy even said hi to me, I'd shrink back to that safe place inside me. I was losing hope that I would ever be able to trust any man again.

Yet God had a plan, and in His own perfect timing He has helped me make the transition from avoiding males to being quite comfortable around them. Little by little, my renewed relationship with my cousins, the dating experiences I did have, and the friendships with guys God blessed me with in high school and college aided my progress tremendously.

Each male friendship healed a part of my broken trust. Their acceptance and care helped release fear's grip. God gradually helped me open up to these friends, and I learned to enjoy the good talks, playful teasing, and sweet laughter in these friendships. I no longer wanted to hide in the dark shadows. I was much closer to the light.

Another level of risk

Within the first week of my sophomore year in college (a small school in Chicago) I met Jay. We quickly became good friends because we had a lot in common, including difficulty trusting others because of our painful pasts. Jay was going through some personal problems, and I jumped at the opportunity to help him. At first, I neither wanted nor expected us to be anything more than friends, so when Jay urged a deeper relationship, I became frightened.

But he was so caring that before long his affection began penetrating the walls around my heart. I trusted Jay, but I was scared and confused. *Should I continue running from a closer relationship or risk it all?* I wondered.

After much thought, I finally took the risk, and we began dating. Jay had so many of the qualities I was looking for in a man. I felt comfortable and safe with him, and we had a lot of fun together. Yet when it came to talking about serious things I would clam up and let him do all the talking. Scared, I began pushing him away, but he wouldn't budge.

"I know you won't let anyone get close, Christa," Jay said. "You think you can live independent of others, but I'm not going to let you do that."

I pushed him back again. "You can share your heart and soul with me, Jay, and I'll be more than willing to listen," I said bluntly, "but there's no way I can ever really open up to you."

I desperately wanted to let down my guard, but memory's chains held me back. It was incredibly frustrating, especially because we both saw potential for this relationship.

In the first few months we fought often: Jay tried desperately to reach the real me, and, out of habit, my fears erected more barriers.

I wanted and needed to open up to Jay, but I honestly didn't know how. I had never allowed myself to need anyone on a deep emotional level. I kept asking him, "What do you want me to say?" I didn't think anyone, including Jay, would be interested in my stories, my family, my friends, and my dreams. So, for a long time I listened to Jay talk, and he waited for me to speak openly to him.

October 1995 (age 19)

The past month has been downright rocky. We get into an average of three fights a week. I'm so used to being the listener that it's hard for me to open up and talk to him, even about trivial things. It's frustrating because there's so much inside that I've been waiting for years to share. Now that I have someone to listen, old fears push him away.

It's incredibly discouraging to find walls still protecting me though I no longer want or need them. I'm too stubborn and independent for my own good, but I don't know how I can change—especially when I thought I had already conquered this. Give me hope, Lord. It is my lifeline.

After a long, difficult struggle I slowly began letting down my defenses. I tested Jay to make sure I could trust him before I became vulnerable in the slightest way. If he made one tiny slip, I would close up again. For instance, if he knew I needed to talk and he didn't take time to draw it out of me or if I revealed something important to me and he brushed it off without thinking, I'd withdraw, assuming he didn't care and that I couldn't trust him.

Light through the crevices

One night Jay and I got into a huge fight because I refused to tell him why it bothered me so much when people said I was quiet. I wanted to tell him, but I couldn't. We were both frustrated.

"Maybe we shouldn't take this relationship any further—if it's going to be all one-sided," Jay ventured. "I'm the only one opening up here."

I was scared of telling anyone my real feelings for fear they wouldn't care about what was important to me. But after a long period of silence, I tried to explain.

"In high school all I ever heard was that I was so quiet—never talked or smiled," I began. "It was maddening because it seemed that by then almost everywhere else but school I was outgoing and talkative. When I hear that I'm quiet it frustrates me because it reminds me that I still have healing to do. For me, being quiet means I'm still hiding, scared to share all that's inside."

Once I started talking, the barricades began to crumble, and I wanted to tell him more. Jay listened intently and drew me out of my shell with questions. Sometimes he had to prod and plead to convince me he really cared about what I was going to say.

I progressed slowly, but at least I was progressing. Each time I shared with Jay and became more transparent, I found I wanted to do it again. I had tasted freedom. How could I go back into my stale and lonely prison? God was faithful, shining His light in the dark crevices, stretching out His hand to touch the part of me that still cowered in the corner. His healing, empowering light helped me begin dismantling those unneeded walls.

I was surprised that talking openly didn't make me feel weak, as I thought it would; it made me feel stronger and more free. In her book *Secret Survivors* E. Sue Blume writes, "Vulnerability is the antithesis of weakness for [risking openness] requires strength and courage . . . To be vulnerable is to be open to the impact of our environment and responsive to others. It leaves you able to be touched by human contact, and capable of feeling all that it brings—joy and pain, sorrow and excitement."[2]

As my relationship with Jay grew, I began to feel he was the only person who truly understood me. I seldom shared deep thoughts and problems with others, but I believed God had brought Jay into my life so I could experience a new level of relationship I'd never known.

> *August 1996 (age 20)*
>
> *I feel more in love with Jay than ever before and know that I want to spend the rest of my life with him if God would so bless me. I feel so comfortable and safe with him. I never thought I'd feel like this with a man after my abuse. God is good.*

Where do we go from here?

By the end of the school year, our relationship had grown serious and we agonized over the thought of spending the entire summer apart. We knew it would somehow be good for us, but we dreaded having to say good-bye. The summer proved to be both torturous and expensive—too many long-distance phone calls! We affirmed our love for each other often and felt sure God meant for us to be together.

Then during summer break, I sensed God calling me to transfer to Northwestern College, a Minnesota Christian college that had a stronger psychology program. I knew the transfer would better prepare me for helping

others, but I agonized over the decision. I wanted to follow God's will, wherever it led, but how could I stand
being 500 miles away from Jay? How could God ask me to
leave the one person I felt He had used to bring such healing to my life?

I vacillated the whole summer, trying to decide what
to do. But I came up with the same conclusion every time—
I needed to transfer.

Jay supported my decision. "You have to follow
God's leading," he said. "As hard as it'll be, somehow we'll
make it through."

Toward the end of summer, I flew out to his home
town to see him. During our visit we talked often about
marriage, feeling strongly that we had a future together.

Back home, I
became overwhelmed with
emotions. I cried at the
thought of all the fun times
we'd had together the past
year, and I cried at the
thought of facing a new
environment without him. I
began second- and third-
guessing my decision to
transfer. I believed God was
calling me to this new school, yet if this was God's will, why
was He making it so hard on me? The thought of facing
another new and strange environment alone flooded me with
waves of fear and depression. I wanted to feel Jay's arms
around me, holding me and making me feel safe.

> *November 25, 1996 (age 20)*
>
> *Jay depends on me a lot. I
> have to be strong for Him,
> but I'm crumbling quickly
> under the pressure. I guess
> when you love someone you'll
> do anything for that person.*

Before school started my family and I went to our cabin for one last vacation. It was good for me to get away from home and distance myself from my doubts and anxieties. Surrounded by God's beautiful creation, I breathed in His peace, strength, and hope, knowing I'd need them to face the uncertainties awaiting me ahead.

The night we got back from vacation—about a week before I had to leave for Northwestern College—Jay called. I was excited to talk to him—until he told me he felt we needed to break up.

[1]Josh McDowell, *In His Image* (San Bernardino: Here's Life Publishers, Inc., 1984), pp. 53–54.
[2]E. Sue Blume, *Secret Survivors,* p. 250.

CHAPTER 10

The Wrong Rock

Find rest, O my soul, in God alone; my hope comes from him.
He alone is my rock and my salvation;
he is my fortress, I will not be shaken.
My salvation and my honor depend on God;
he is my mighty rock, my refuge.
Trust in him at all times, O people;
pour out your hearts to him, for God is our refuge.
Psalm 62:5–8

When Jay called, he said the Lord had been working within him, and he felt we needed to break up because we weren't putting God first in our relationship.

I was in complete shock. After a year of working hard to freely open up to Jay, why would the Lord do this?

The timing was horrible. How could I face the unknown at a new school the following week? It scared me. The more we talked, the more my heart broke.

"I don't know what the future holds," he said, "but I need to follow God's will."

Terribly hurt, I reverted to my old self-preservation mode and tried to hide the pain that vulnerability had brought again. But I couldn't keep from crying. I hung up the phone in bitter tears.

Shaking, I went upstairs to talk to Mom and Dad. "Jay and I just broke up," I blurted through my tears.

Dad held me as I told them what happened, and they both tried to console me. But I never thought love could hurt that bad.

"I don't understand why this is happening," I kept saying through my sobs. "I can't go through with transferring to Northwestern. It's too much right now."

"Yes, you can," Dad assured me. "You've already been through so much, but you've come through stronger for it. You're a fighter, Christa."

"I'm sick of fighting," I cried. "I want some peace and rest."

I felt angry at Jay for pushing me to trust him and fall in love with him. I no longer trusted him, God, or myself. I felt angry at God for allowing me to go through the long process of opening up, only to have it end so painfully. I asked God why. That night I wrote in my journal:

Intellectually I know that adversity builds character,

but enough already! I feel like I haven't stopped fighting since I was abused. I know doing God's will is best and that some of life's greatest treasures come through suffering, but it's hard to get my heart to believe that now. I feel empty, raw, and completely out of control, and I hate it. Jay was so much a part of my life that I can't imagine him not being in it. I don't know how to go on. I've cried out to God, praying that He will guide me in His path and fill me with His peace, comfort, and hope. But so far—nothing.

True test of faith

Desperate to connect with my heavenly Father, I began reading the Bible, looking for answers, guidance, and reassurance, but I didn't sense His presence. I felt there was a stone where my heart once had been.

"God," I prayed, "I'm going to trust you through all this and not let Satan win—not after all the progress I've

---

September 5, 1996 (age 20)

I feel so off-center. Jay was my rock, my strength, and my best friend. I cry in anguish to You, God, to fill Jay's place—the place You should have had from the start. This heart-wrenching pain has finally taken me to where I should have been all along—in Your Word. I'm holding onto the promises I'm reading there, but I feel my heart will break into a million pieces. I know Your ways are not my ways, and Your will is perfect. I must let You be in charge—as hard as that is right now. Please carry me because I'm having trouble finding my way.

made." This was the true test of faith—to trust a God I couldn't see, hear, or feel. Believing that somehow God had a reason for this and that His ultimate good would far outweigh the pain of this breakup, I began looking for what that might be.

Gradually I saw two good things come out of this new pain: opening up to my parents, and a new empathy.

- I reached out to my Mom and Dad when I was hurting, and they comforted me. I loved the warmth and affection of being in my dad's arms, and I could finally talk with my parents about men. This was definitely progress.

- After this experience I could also better relate to the youth I longed to work with. How could I ever understand someone else's broken heart if mine had never broken?

I wrote in my journal:

> God, keep showing me the positives, and please don't let me close my heart to the love of others. That would be safe, but I would never again experience the sweet joy of that precious gift.

A jealous God

I was scared when I got to Northwestern College and faced unfamiliar surroundings without Jay for support, but God filled my empty heart with an incredible peace I'd never known before (see Philippians 4:7).

Everything, from my class work to my professors to the students and staff I met, confirmed my decision to transfer there. My faith in God had been so weak, and I began to

realize why. God is a jealous God, and He wanted to be the Center of my life. The truth was difficult to face. Jay and I had worn each other out, depending on each other for needs that only God—the Source of Life—could meet.

Invisible red flags

As I struggled to make God top priority in my life, I began to see several reasons why my "perfect relationship" with Jay had been, in reality, an unhealthy attachment.

- *Based on need.* The focus from the very beginning was not two people trying to get to know each other. It was my trying to help Jay with his problems and his trying to help me with mine. At the time, it seemed safe. Because someone needed me, I could be in control to a certain extent.

Looking back, I can see signs from the beginning that something was wrong. But I ignored the red flags. I loved being needed. So when we broke up, I was scared I would never find another person to open up to, and I was scared Jay might.

- *Too much too soon.* To be honest, we built our relationship so quickly that there wasn't a solid foundation on which to stand. The school year had barely started before Jay and I—two strangers—began dating, were professing our love for each other, and started dreaming of a future together.

- *Lack of boundaries.* "Boundaries are violated when one person takes false, unnecessary, or excessive responsibility for the other . . . when one partner clings excessively to another," write Drs. Hemfelt, Minirth, and Meier.

The closeness Jay and I developed soon limited my personal freedom. Every decision I made involved him, and he got upset when I spent time alone or with other friends. I was so concerned about taking care of Jay that I didn't take care of myself. For instance, I found it difficult to say no to him when he called at all hours, saying he needed me.

Our breakup was especially traumatic because my identity was wrapped up in Jay. I believed I couldn't survive without him. He was my life. At school I wasn't an individual. I was half of a couple. This friendship that I thought had built me up in Christ actually swallowed me whole. Somehow, in the excitement, I lost myself. And the scary part is that for a long time I didn't even know I was missing.

- *Exclusiveness.* My focus was on Jay. Therefore I had little energy for other relationships, including my relationship with God.

- *Defensiveness.* Whenever my friends urged caution, I became defensive. Blind to how unhealthy it had become for Jay to consume more and more of my life, I became angry at my friends, further alienating myself from them.

Cries for mercy

But God graciously opened my eyes, and I cried for mercy, wisdom, and discernment to find balance for healthy future relationships. I didn't want to go back to those old emotional barriers—which was my gut reaction—and I also needed to learn how to take care of myself.

Not only was I looking to another person to fill me and make me whole, but I was taking too much responsibility for another's life without realizing how unhealthy that was. I didn't equate trying to buoy his spirits and solve his problems with my ever-decreasing energy levels. What had started out as a year full of promise and zeal turned into one of the hardest years of my life. My world seemed to be falling apart, and I had neither the strength nor the energy to stop it.

Even three weeks after school ended, it was all I could do to get out of bed. My mom convinced me to go to the doctor, but he couldn't find any physical cause for my fatigue. I didn't realize until later that my dependence on Jay had drained me both spiritually and emotionally. I gave all I could give until I ran dry (see Jeremiah 17:5–6).

Leaning on others and letting them lean on us, I've learned, isn't wrong as long as we first turn to our heavenly Father and lean on Him. After all, He is the Healer. We are only His healing agents. But I hadn't been doing that.

Idolatry?

While I was dating Jay, my relationship with God also deteriorated. Jay quickly replaced God as the Rock and center of my life. Many times I tried to get back on track, but I failed again and again and couldn't understand why.

After we broke up God gently revealed to me that Jay had become an idol in my life. Before, whenever I read Scriptures warning about worshiping idols or false gods, I skipped over those verses, believing they didn't apply to me. But Alan Redpath says that our god is the person we think is the most precious.[1]

Jay had become more precious to me than God— my Creator, my heavenly Father, the One who—more than

November 25, 1996 (age 20)

Can I ever get me back? Will I ever be whole again? Or is that what love is about, constantly giving of ourselves as we continually turn to God to fill us with Himself, who is love itself? I don't want to come to the point where I'm empty and have nothing left to give. I'm so scared to trust again. Where's the balance, Lord? I don't want to hurt, but I don't want to miss out on love! My fears are great, but I know I have to endure the pain and risk trusting again. God, lead me forward. I desire to follow you anywhere you want me to go.

anyone else—loves me and yearns to spend time with me. I was worshiping an idol! No wonder I had quit growing spiritually.

Through the prophet Jeremiah, God says, "My people have committed two sins: They have forsaken me, the spring of living water, and have dug their own cisterns, broken cisterns that cannot hold water" (Jeremiah 2:13). I had turned my back on God, the only One who could supply me with Living Water, and tried to find life in a human being (who was just as broken and weak as me) to meet my deep, inner needs.

How silly we must look to God as we desperately try to fill the vacuum inside us with people or things instead of Him. Yet how patiently He waits for us to confess it, and then He forgives us and welcomes us back into His loving arms.

In my heartache, I came to the end of myself—exactly where I needed to be. I had stepped backward into the pit, but all I had to do was reach up and grasp the loving hand that wanted to pull me out. As I did, I quickly began discovering what trusting is all about.

Relearning trust in God

In his book *Inside Out* Dr. Larry Crabb writes, "Tough faith never grows in a comfortable mind. But it can develop nicely when our mind is so troubled by confusion that we either believe God or give up on life."[2]

I knew that place. I remember one night, shortly after Jay and I broke up, my overwhelming despair brought back old thoughts that life wasn't worth living. I cried out to the Lord, "God, by faith I know you're here, that you love me, and that your plan is perfect. I hate what's happening right now, but I know that you are good and merciful, so I'm going to trust completely in you to save me from drowning in all this sorrow and to make me into the person you want me to become. If, in one year, I cannot look back and see growth that's taken place both personally and spiritually, I quit. You alone are my hope, I have nothing left but you."

God heard my plea. Though my emotions fought my will to trust God, I determined to depend completely on Him. He wanted to be first in my life, and He helped me begin a new journey, discovering what trusting Him is all about. It was no longer enough for me to pursue healing; I wanted to pursue the Healer and come to know who God is, not just what He does. I was ready to learn how to truly trust Him again.

In my quest, I became passionate about building a rock-solid relationship with Christ, believing that if my relationship with God was strong, then everything else would fall into place (see Matthew 6:33). I knew my comfort, joy, and peace rested in Him alone.

Frustrated by how limited my knowledge of Him was, I hungrily read the Bible daily. Now my heart no longer felt like stone, and God opened my eyes to scriptural truths that hadn't made sense before. I got excited as He began speaking directly to me through His Word, replacing my hurt with His joy. Every day I depended on His Word for the comfort, strength, and reassurance I needed. It truly became "a lamp to my feet and a light for my path" (Psalm 119:105), guiding me out of the darkness.

> I consider everything a loss compared to the surpassing greatness of knowing Christ Jesus my Lord, for whose sake I have lost all things. I consider them rubbish, that I may gain Christ.
>
> PHILIPPIANS 3:8

I also began to understand that my relationship with God could grow only if I spent regular time with Him, talking to Him as well as listening. So prayer also became a part of my daily routine. I poured out my heart to God, believing, by faith, that prayer is powerful and that His answers would be the best—even if they weren't what I had hoped. God became my refuge, giving me rest midst the storm and a perfect peace that contradicted all logic in my circumstances.

A case of surrender

I still didn't understand why I had to go through so much pain. Some insights on suffering would come later. But knowing God was in control, I held tightly to Proverbs 3:5–6: "Trust in the LORD with all your heart and lean not on your own understanding; in all your ways acknowledge him, and he will make your paths straight."

My brokenness made me more certain than ever before that God is real, that He is the Source of Life, and that He would use my broken heart to bring me closer to Him. I let go of everything I had, including my wounded spirit, and gave it to Him to heal and eventually use. God said, "Be still, and know that I am God" (Psalm 46:10).

And I surrendered.

Having come to the end of myself, I let Him be the One in control, knowing that God was now where He should have been all along—in the driver's seat. And as I surrendered, He granted me more peace. After getting far off track, thinking of Jay as my rock, I discovered this reminder in God's Word: "God alone . . . is my rock and my salvation; he is my fortress [my walls of protection], I will not be shaken . . . he is my mighty rock, my refuge. Trust in him at all times" (Psalm 62:5–8, bracketed text mine).

A childlike trust

God began showing me that trusting Him was quite simple. I thought back to what He had been teaching me about the "child within." Adults, in their self-sufficiency find more difficulty in learning trust because they have a choice. Children, on the other hand, don't have a choice. They must trust and depend on others for everything. Childlike trust in God is an unquestioning belief that He's in charge—we are not—and He wants only the best for us.

Again I had to become like a child—humble, honest, open, real, dependent—so my heavenly Father could meet my needs. He knew me better than anyone, and I could trust Him.

As I did, what had been a limited faith based on what God was doing in me became a permanent core trust in God solely because He is good—whether or not He does what I think is best for me. God was producing in me a faith that would endure.

Oswald Chambers writes, "The very things we try to avoid and fight against—tribulation, suffering, and persecution—are the very things that produce abundant joy in us"[3] (see 2 Corinthians 7:4). Though I was still hurting, I found a deep joy by focusing on God.

God-dependency

As my faith grew, I found true security in depending on Him. At times I tried to regain control and hide behind self-protection walls when I thought I might face pain again. But the Lord confronted me with my sin of fearful self-protection and self-sufficiency. Dan Allender writes, "Self-protection makes a great deal of sense at the moment, but it is the opposite of faith in God."

I had spent most of my life pretending I was strong and didn't need anyone else. Now God was telling me that true strength is admitting my weaknesses and allowing God's power to manifest itself through them (see 2 Corinthians 12:8–10).

When I am the weakest, God's power is most evident, so I don't have to be ashamed of my weaknesses or wear myself out trying to look strong.

One day, while I was reading my Bible, it hit me that even Jesus Himself didn't act self-sufficient. First of all, He depended on God the Father for everything, and then He

> *January 7, 1997 (age 20)*
>
> *I'm thankful God has gotten me to the place of brokenness where I can see how weak and helpless I am without God leading the way. I hate facing it, but I don't think I've ever been healthier. Dear God, please help me let go of all things, including Jay, and hold tightly only to You.*

relied on other people to help Him when He needed it. We see it clearly in the last hours of His life. While praying in the Garden of Gethsemane, facing imminent death, He asked His disciples to stay with Him—He needed their support (see Matthew 26:38). In the Gospel of Mark, at the scene of the crucifixion, Mark points out women from Galilee standing by who "had followed him and cared for his needs" (Mark 15:41). He allowed them to take care of Him.

I called myself a follower of Jesus, yet I wasn't following His example. Instead, I'd chosen self-sufficiency and independence over trust and interdependence. Eventually I had to admit that I needed other people. God created all of us with a need for relationships, and I needed to share my story with others and accept the love and support they offered.

A relationship (with Walter) had caused my deepest pain, and it was through relationships (with God, family, and friends) that the Lord ultimately brought the healing I needed.

Crisis of the heart

We all struggle sometimes with dependence on the Lord because we're fallen people, but abuse victims find it even more difficult to completely rely on Him. When we can't trust other people, how can we trust God? We can't even see Him, and we may still blame Him for not stopping the abuse. Since that cruelty left us feeling powerless, how can we willingly hand over our desire for control, surrendering everything to Him?

For all my professed trust in God, I secretly wanted control of my own life, somehow believing that I, the created, knew better than my Creator what was best for me. This crisis of the heart was a test of my faith: Did I really believe all that I claimed to believe?

Good ultimately came out of my relationship with Jay—even though we ended up following different paths. The Lord has brought me to the place where I can willingly give Him the bricks of my self-protective wall, choosing openness and trust rather than fear and self-imprisonment. Only He could bring new life from the painful death of a relationship.

Opening my heart to people was a risk, but to shut myself off from love and care would take me back to the deadness I'd fought so hard to lose. I cried out to God, asking Him to help me trust people and establish healthy boundaries. I wanted to live life fully as God intended. He graciously surrounded me with caring friends and taught me to reach out to them whenever I had a need.

I still struggle sometimes with trust, feeling the urge to curl up in a ball, retreat from life, and be safe. But I'm learning to trust in God for my safety instead of hiding from everyone in fear.

Finding myself again

For the longest time, having put so much into an unhealthy relationship, I struggled with the sickening thought that I had lost more than I gained. But I now know that God used that year of pain and joy mingled together to put me on the road to God-dependency. It was a year in which what I knew to be true in my head became my passion, the core belief I based my life on. (I know I'll be traveling that God-dependency road the rest of my life, continually striving to surrender to Him.) And through it all, I again fell in love—this time with Jesus Christ, my Lord and Savior, and my best friend.

One of my greatest gains was finding myself again. As I began to separate who I was from my enmeshment with Jay, I gained confidence, grew more assertive and less self-conscious, finally becoming comfortable with myself—faults and all. I was finally in the light—His Light—as I experienced true freedom and a new passion for life.

God has restored my dignity and helped me to accept myself as a beloved child of God. My self-esteem is no longer based on meeting needs or on what others, like Jay, think of me. Rather my identity is in Christ. I don't need to be in a human love relationship to like myself or feel secure. Paul reminds us, "You are complete in Him" (Colossians 2:10 NKJV).

My faith in God grows even stronger when I look back on that year that began with such heartache and confusion and see how He walked with me on a secure path. I had

---

July 16, 1997 (age 21)

After talking with a friend tonight I realized again God's amazing faithfulness. As I look back on the last year of my life, I see God's hand clearly guiding me through tough times. What began as one of the worst years of my life has turned out to be the best. God has a way of turning life's junk into the most beautiful things.

And it all began almost one year ago on an anguish-filled night when I made a decision of the will to choose faith in an unseen God rather than believe Satan's lies that life was not worth living. We serve a living God who answers prayer and is close to the broken-hearted! God was faithful in bringing me here to Northwestern. He knew the changes I needed to make, the lessons I needed to learn, and the people I needed to meet. It's amazing how God works. His plan is perfect.

---

fallen away from my first love (Revelation 2:4), looking for identity and security from the wrong source, but when I took a step of faith, admitted I was powerless to heal myself, and willingly handed control of my life to God, I found Him quietly waiting to be the Rock I needed.

But would I ever understand why God allowed all this pain in the first place? And could I ever truly forgive Walter for what he did?

Addictive Love Says . . .

1. I can't live without you. You give my life meaning.

2. You make me feel valuable. When I'm with you, I am somebody.

3. I can't make it on my own.

4. I want you to be a total part of my life, and I want to be a total part of yours.

5. All of the hard times are worth the good times. I will be here forever, no matter what happens.

6. I can't bear to think of you sharing your thoughts and feelings with someone else. You are the only one who has ever understood me.

7. You should be sensitive to my needs. I have feelings, you know, and I need you to take that into consideration.

8. If you really care, you will treat me the way I need to be treated to feel good.

Authentic Love Says . . .

1. I can live without you, but I choose not to.

2. I am a valuable person, and you affirm that value to me.

3. I can make it on my own. Having you as part of my life makes it easier.

4. We are two separate people with individual lives to lead. I encourage you to pursue your interests, and I will pursue mine. This kind of space and diversity is good for us.

5. Love should seek another's highest good. To the best of my ability, I will do that for you.

6. We are richer for sharing our lives with other people. I encourage you to have other close relationships.

7. Mutuality is the glue that holds us together. I enjoy you, and in that enjoyment many of my needs for importance, belonging, and intimacy are met.

8. I will accept the way you show me you care about me. Sometimes I may have to ask you about your actions, but generally, I will take at face value what you say and do.[4]

[1]Alan Redpath from his book *The Ten Commandments,* quoted in *The Great Compromise* by Greg Laurie (Dallas: Word, 1994), p. 75.

[2]Dr. Larry Crabb, *Inside Out* (Colorado Springs: NavPress, 1988), p. 107.

[3]Oswald Chambers, *My Utmost for His Highest* (Grand Rapids: Discovery House Publishers, 1992), August 29.

[4]Jan Silvious, *Please Don't Say You Need Me* (Grand Rapids: Zondervan Publishing House, 1989), pp. 123-124.

Encouragement for those rebuilding their trust in God:
When you're not sure if God is trustworthy . . .

Proverbs 29:25 "Fear of man will prove to be a snare, but whoever trusts in the LORD is kept safe."

Psalms 9:10 "You, LORD, have never forsaken those who seek you."

Deuteronomy 31:8 "The LORD himself goes before you and will be with you; he will never leave you nor forsake you. Do not be afraid; do not be discouraged."

Isaiah 50:10 "Let him who walks in the dark, who has no light, trust in the name of the Lord and rely on his God."

When you want to trust God but you're not sure you can . . .

Psalm 37:4–7 "Delight yourself in the LORD and he will give you the desires of your heart. Commit your way to the LORD; trust in him and he will do this: He will make your righteousness shine like the dawn, the justice of your cause like the noonday sun. Be still before the Lord and wait patiently for him."

Hebrews 11:1 "Now faith is being sure of what we hope for and certain of what we do not see."

Jeremiah 17:7–8 "Blessed is the man who trusts in the Lord, whose confidence is in him. He will be like a tree planted by the water that sends out its roots by the stream. It does not fear when heat comes; its leaves are always green. It has no worries."

When you're not sure God will hear you when you call . . .

Psalm 34:15 "The eyes of the LORD are on the righteous and his ears are attentive to their cry."

Psalm 10:17 "You hear, O LORD, the desire of the afflicted; you encourage them, and you listen to their cry."

Psalm 34:17–18 "The righteous cry out, and the LORD hears them; he delivers them from all their troubles. The LORD is close to the brokenhearted and saves those who are crushed in spirit."

Isaiah 65:24 "Before they call I will answer; while they are still speaking I will hear."

Exodus 22:23, 27 "If . . . they cry out to me, I will certainly hear their cry. . . . I will hear for I am compassionate."

When you feel too weak to try anymore . . .

2 Corinthians 1:8–10 "We were under great pressure, far beyond our ability to endure, so that we despaired even of life. Indeed, in our hearts we felt the sentence of death. But this happened that we might not rely on ourselves but on God, who raises the dead. He has delivered us from such a deadly peril, and he will deliver us. On him we have set our hope that he will continue to deliver us.

Psalm 125:1–2 "Those who trust in the Lord are like Mount Zion, which cannot be shaken but endures forever. As the mountains surround Jerusalem, so the Lord surrounds his people both now and forevermore."

When you think you can't let go of whatever stands in the way of trusting God . . .

Exodus 20:3–5 "You shall have no other gods before me. You shall not make for yourself an idol in the form of anything . . . for I, the LORD your God, am a jealous God."

Psalm 118:8 "It is better to take refuge in the LORD than to trust in man."

1 Chronicles 16:11 "Look to the LORD and his strength; seek his face always."

Mark 12:30 "Love the Lord your God with all your heart and with all your soul and with all your mind and with all your strength."

Philippians 4:13 "I can do everything through him who gives me strength."

CHAPTER 11

Suffering and Forgiveness

*We also rejoice in our sufferings, because we know that suffering
produces perseverance; perseverance, character; and character,
hope. And hope does not disappoint us,
because God has poured out his love into our hearts
by the Holy Spirit, whom he has given us.*

Romans 5:3-5

Does God's Word talk about all the suffering that
results from sexual abuse?

Yes. When I read Tamar's story, I thought it was one
of the saddest stories in the Bible. Tamar was a young woman
who was raped by Amnon, her half brother (see 2 Samuel 13).
Both were children of the great King David of Israel.

I could relate to Tamar's suffering in several ways:

- She was violated in her own home.

- Her abuser was someone she trusted.

- Her innocence was cruelly stolen.

- The abuse changed the course of her life.

- The abuser resorted to denial and refused to take responsibility for his sin.

Unlike me, however, Tamar told her story right away. And apparently she didn't receive the support she desperately needed. Her brother Absalom and her father were both angry, but they did nothing to hold Amnon responsible. Although Absalom took Tamar into his home, the Bible says she lived there, "a desolate woman."

A classic case

The story reads like a classic case of sexual abuse—the stealing of her dignity, the denial within the families, and the devastation of her shame and grief. However, Tamar chose not to hide but to publicly expose what Amnon did to her: "Tamar put ashes on her head and tore the ornamented robe she was wearing. She put her hand on her head and went away, weeping aloud as she went" (v. 19).

Like many victims' family members, Absalom tried to cover up, minimize, and deny the effects of the abuse. He told Tamar to bury her feelings and the memory: "Be quiet now, my sister," he said. "[Amnon] is your brother. Don't take this thing to heart" (v. 20).

How could she not take this horrifying betrayal to heart? Forced silence in the midst of unresolved bitterness, grief, and anger destroys a person.

Amnon received no punishment from David for hurting this precious daughter of the king. David had mastered the "art" of covering up sexual immorality. Tamar's story appears only one chapter after David's adultery with Bathsheba and the subsequent murder of her husband to cover up that sin. Ironically, when Absalom kills Amnon, David grieves for the abuser—his son. But apparently he never grieves for the hurts of the victim, his daughter.

This true story sounds a wake-up call: Stop ignoring the destruction that abuse causes.

Yet God is mysteriously silent in the account of Tamar's suffering. Where was God when she was being betrayed, abused, ignored, and made to endure years of silent agony and despair?

I've asked similar questions—over and over—about my own abuse and heartaches. Where was God when Walter repeatedly abused me? Why did He allow a family friend to mess up my whole life for a few moments of depraved pleasure? Where was God when I got to college and thought I had discovered my true love but found only more hurt?

Answers vs. insights

In fact, why does anyone have to suffer at all? Theologians and other scholars have debated this question for centuries. For all my wrestling with it, I certainly don't have the ultimate explanation. Answers may remain elusive for a reason, however.

Through my painful journey, I believe I've gained a broader understanding that comes only with experience. I don't have all the answers, but I've found peace in the midst of the questions. God has comforted me through some insights about His Son, and I've been learning to trust Him all over again:

1. Jesus knows exactly what it's like to experience pain and despair. He was also a victim who suffered because of other people's sins. Jesus understands my anguish, fears, and grief for He felt these emotions too as He faced crucifixion. In that darkest hour He cried, "My soul is overwhelmed with sorrow to the point of death" (Mark 14:34).

2. Jesus understands my many tormented cries to God for mercy. In a heart-wrenching prayer, He pleaded, "'Father, if you are willing, take this cup from me; yet not my will, but yours be done' . . . And being in anguish, he prayed more earnestly, and his sweat was like drops of blood falling to the ground" (Luke 22:42, 44).

3. Jesus knows what it's like to be alone and rejected. "He was despised and rejected by men, a man of sorrows, and familiar with suffering. Like one from whom men hide their faces he was despised, and we esteemed him not" (Isaiah 53:3).

4. Jesus was horribly betrayed by a friend—by several of them. Judas handed Him over to His executioners, Peter claimed he never knew Jesus,

and all His of followers ran away in fear when
Jesus needed them most.

5. Jesus knows what it's like to feel abandoned—
   when it seems as if everyone, including God,
   is silent. From the cross, Jesus cried out in agony,
   "My God, my God, why have you forsaken me?"
   (Mark 15:34).

6. Jesus knows what it's like to feel weak and stripped
   of dignity. He was flogged and nailed onto a rough
   cross where He hung naked for all to see. He understands my shame, for He suffered the shame of others
   as well. At the cross God placed the weight of the
   world on Jesus' shoulders. Then and there Christ truly
   understood my suffering. He took my burdens and
   made them His own on that cross (Isaiah 53:4).

Jesus had traveled the path of suffering I was on.
Who better to comfort a weary traveler than someone who
has already endured the treacherous journey?

Sharing in His sufferings

I began to see that my own deep pain could help me
identify with Christ and what He went through to accomplish
our redemption. I don't think we can begin to comprehend
the events of the cross unless we ourselves have suffered deeply.

Paul's number one passion was this: "I want to know
Christ and the power of his resurrection and the fellowship
of sharing in his sufferings, becoming like him in his death"
(Philippians 3:10–11). I didn't understand that passion until
I reflected upon my own pain in the light of Christ's.

I desperately wanted to become closer to Him, to become one with Him—and my suffering was drawing me there. None of us will never feel the depths of utter desolation that Jesus felt on the cross, but when I read the prophecy of Jesus being "cut off from the land of the living" (Isaiah 53:8), I recalled the deadness I sensed for so many years. And when I read that Jesus was "the resurrection and the life" (John 11:25), I thanked Him for restoring my joy and passion for living.

Jesus calls us to be like Him, yet somehow we try to do that without being wounded or bearing scars. Paul's threefold desire—to know Christ, the power of His resurrection, and the fellowship of His sufferings—are all interconnected. We cannot attain one without the others.

He understands our pain better than anyone and grieves with us, so "let us fix our eyes on Jesus, the author and perfecter of our faith, who for the joy set before him endured the cross, scorning its shame, and sat down at the right hand of the throne of God. Consider him who endured such opposition from sinful men, so that you will not grow weary and lose heart" (Hebrews 12:2–3). Frankly, not having Jesus stand by us in times of suffering would be the most crushing sorrow of all.

My own pain helped me enter into fellowship with Him. He was wounded so that I could know His resurrection power—now and for eternity. His wounds had a purpose—the salvation of our souls. And so do ours—even though we may not see it immediately. No longer a victim, Jesus triumphed over suffering. If God can transform the evil done to Christ on the cross into the best gift for all humanity, surely we can trust Him to transform our pain into a thing of glory (Romans 8:31–32).

What a great insight this was for me! I can live in the victory of Christ's triumph over sin and death because He—the Source of my faith—has felt every painful moment of my life.

A refining process

Satan seeks to destroy us with painful trials, but God uses those very things to refine, strengthen, and make us more usable for Him. He says, "See, I have refined you, though not as silver; I have tested you in the furnace of affliction" (Isaiah 48:10).

When God is silent, the future looks dark, and we can't see an end to our problems, Satan would like nothing better than for us to give up. Yet God calls us to persevere because pain refines us (James 1:2–4).

Longing for Home

Someday Jesus will come back to fight and win a final battle against all evil. All who have accepted Him as Lord and Savior will live with Him for eternity. In heaven there will be no more grieving as He wipes every tear from our eyes (see Revelation 21:4).

I had always hoped Jesus would wait to return until I had accomplished all my dreams. But with my new perspective on suffering, I started looking forward to His coming. I had been living as if I were already home, but I began to see that heaven is my Home.

I've often ached for something better than this life. Now I understand why. As a Christian, I sometimes feel uncomfortable and out of place here because I'm only a stranger passing through. The Bible often refers to God's people as strangers and aliens in this world (e.g., 1 Peter 2:11).

The more I live as though I'm already Home—hoping for peace, security, and ultimate happiness here on earth—the farther I am from God. My joy and peace come from God alone who's preparing a place for me in heaven. And one day I'll find complete fulfillment there—without pain—for all eternity (see Isaiah 65:17–19 and 2 Corinthians 5:6). But until then suffering is inevitable. The Bible teaches that we should expect it (see John 16:33). When the storms come, those who have made Christ their Rock and foundation will not be destroyed (Matthew 7:24–27).

Perhaps God chooses not to alleviate all suffering so we'll never forget where our real Home is. The apostle Paul writes, "Do not lose heart. . . . Inwardly we are being renewed day by day. For our light and momentary troubles are achieving for us an eternal glory that far outweighs them all" (2 Corinthians 4:16–17).

Looking at life through eternal eyes puts my suffering here on earth in perspective and helps me persevere until God chooses to take me Home (Romans 8:18).

Knowing God is in control

Why must we suffer? I don't know.

Why was I abused? I don't know.

But I do know that God wants us to completely trust Him, to believe that He is ultimately in control even when evil seems to be winning more battles than good does. Even when He is silent, He is not deaf to our cries for mercy.

He's always there helping us heal and grow through the pain, making us strong, firm, and steadfast (1 Peter 5:10).

Tamar was not alone, and neither are we. I now know that God was with me all those nights long ago, crying the tears I had deep inside and feeling my pain as if it were His own (Isaiah 63:9).

Pain truly refines our faith if we allow Him to skim off the impurities and make us more like Him. I believe that because I determined not to let my suffering be for nothing, God developed in me a compassion and perseverance I never would have known otherwise. He has been faithful through it all, and the more I remembered that, the more I could trust Him for the next difficult task—forgiveness.

> SOME REMINDERS ABOUT SUFFERING
>
> - God doesn't cause suffering. He allows it.
> - Suffering exists in this world because of the sin that entered our world through Adam and Eve.
> - God has given us free will to make our own choices which often affect innocent people.
> - Our finite minds see suffering from a limited perspective. We must trust in the one who sees and knows all things.

Accepting the refining work of suffering in my life was one thing. But forgiving my abuser was quite another. Forgive and forget?

I remember the first time my parents asked me if I would ever be able to forgive Walter. My first thought was,

Why should I? He doesn't deserve it!

I thought that if I forgave him, I would be excusing his behavior, and I wanted to make him pay. Even though I rarely saw the man, I nursed my bitter hatred, hoping that somehow I was harming him. But my loathing wasn't hurting Walter. It was hurting me. Bitterness took its toll—emotionally and spiritually—until I understood that by not forgiving my abuser I was letting Satan win. Walter still had power over me that he didn't realize he had.

I had yearned so long to escape the darkness and find the light. But one day this verse rebuked me: "Anyone who claims to be in the light but hates his brother is still in the darkness" (1 John 2:9).

Like so many other things along this healing journey, I found that forgiveness is a process that takes time. It's usually one of the last issues survivors face because we need to understand what needs to be forgiven. We need to feel, express, and let go of the anger. When we do, we release the abuser's hold on us.

Getting untrapped

Rich Buhler gives this perspective in his book *Pain and Pretending*: "Do you see that if you elect to live your life confined and imprisoned by what has happened to you, you are trapped? For you to do the unexpected—to forgive your abuser—is to be free of him and what he has done to you."[1]

The choice was up to me. I knew I needed to forgive—not only for myself but because God commands us to forgive everyone who has hurt us. He says our refusal to forgive is sin and that an unforgiving spirit has ugly consequences

Fall 1996 (age 20)

*The other day I was reading Luke 8:49-56, which depicts Jesus'
miracle of bringing a dead girl back to life. I've been thinking
about this, a lot. God seems to be saying to me, "Christa, I did
the same for you. I restored you and gave you life because I love
you and I want you to see that there is more to the human experience than merely enduring."*

*The abuse I suffered resulted in an emotional and spiritual death
that lasted for years, yet there was hope. For just as Jesus said
of the girl, "She is not dead but asleep," He was saying of me, "I
will not give up on her for she is only sleeping. I will wake her
and give her life."*

*I see now how faithful God is! He did just that. He raised my
lifeless spirit to Himself and breathed new life into me. I've
awakened to a life I've never known before and a God Who is
more real and loving than I'd ever imagined. The veil has been
lifted, and I'm experiencing life with a new depth and vitality
without my abuse distorting the view. My loving Father has
performed a healing miracle, transforming my life from darkness and despair to light and hope. I'm discovering what is
truly important in life and place a high value on treasured
relationships.*

(e.g., Matthew 18:21–35). Yet I felt God was asking too much from me. How could I let go of all the pain and anger, the regrets of wasted years spent coping with the effects of his violation?

I tried to avoid Walter, but every time I saw him I shrank within myself in shame and disgust. I viewed him as evil and couldn't imagine ever feeling the compassion my parents had for him.

Over time God reminded me of Jesus' words as He was being crucified: "Father, forgive them, for they do not know what they are doing" (Luke 23:34). He drew on His Father's strength to forgive His abusers as they mocked and tortured Him.

I knew God expected the same from me, even if Walter never fully understood the devastation of his actions. Jesus, our example, never asks us to do anything that He has not done already. "Be kind and compassionate to one another," Scripture says, "forgiving each other, just as in Christ God forgave you" (Ephesians 4:32).

We can't wait to forgive until we feel like it because that time will never come. Forgiveness is an act of the will, a deliberate choice of obedience. But the Lord knows we can't possibly do it on our own. If we're willing, He works it out in us.

Lavishing grace

One day, as I was thinking about Jesus' suffering on the cross, it hit me that Jesus died for both Walter's sins and my own. I was not responsible for the abuse, but I was guilty of other sins for which Jesus gave up His life.

Two important truths touched my heart:

1. I am a sinner, just like Walter, in need of God's saving grace. I am no better than he is, even if his sin caused me a tremendous amount of pain. I've hurt people, too, and I need to be forgiven for those sins. Walter could never repay me for all my wounds and losses, but I could never repay the debt I owe God, either. Knowing this doesn't lessen the pain, but it gives a better perspective.

2. God loves Walter, just as He loves me. That doesn't mean He's not angry for all the pain my abuser caused. Jesus vividly demonstrated His anger at the sin done against children: "If anyone causes one of these little ones who believe in me to sin [or stop trusting God], it would be better for him to have a large millstone hung around his neck and to be drowned in the depths of the sea" (Matthew 18:6, bracketed text mine). Yet no matter what sins we each have committed, our God is a God of love, and He wants everyone to come to know Him. That's why He sent Jesus to pay the penalty for our sin.

He didn't have to do that. But the apostle Paul says God lavished His grace on us. (Ephesians 1:7–8) The gift of grace leaves the recipient one responsibility—to extend grace to others. But how?

I eventually came to the point that I wanted to forgive Walter, but I didn't know how. Once I was willing, God showed me that I must depend on His help through the process. Forgiving wasn't a one-time event. Over a period of several months, I prayed that God would help me forgive and let go of the bitterness. I tried but became frustrated, thinking I'd never be able to do it.

Yet the day came when I noticed my attitude toward my abuser changing. God was working in my heart. When I saw Walter, I no longer saw that evil, powerful monster that had haunted my nightmares. Instead I saw a deeply hurting man who needed help. Hatred and bitterness slowly started yielding to compassion.

I no longer felt afraid of him, either. Having suffered enough from his sin, I had begun to release the hold he had over me. Forgiveness was a gift of freedom—a gift I was giving myself.

That didn't mean forgetting the abuse happened or never feeling anger toward him again. In our human nature, these feelings return. But for me they've come in decreasing waves, and God is helping me let go of them.

The question of reconciliation

Forgiveness doesn't necessarily mean reconciliation between the abuser and survivor. Reconciliation certainly can't be forced, and it may not be safe. Forgiving an abuser doesn't mean we have to automatically trust that person again, either. Trust is earned, and setting limits on relationships is healthy. But whether reconciliation happens or not, survivors can still find wholeness.

I believe that reconciliation is impossible without help from above.

Personally, I no longer wanted contact with Walter. Believing that if I ever did talk to him he would deny the abuse ever happened, I resolved to move on, trusting God to make me whole and complete. And I decided to let God, the Ultimate Judge, take care of Walter.

There was no point in trying to get back at him. Revenge is not sweet, and it was not mine to take (Romans 12:19). Walter will one day stand before God who will review each sin committed. Justice will be served.

But there's a difference between seeking revenge and seeking justice—taking an abuser, who committed a criminal offense, to court in hope of protecting other children. The law demands that offenders pay for their crime. Forgiveness does not erase the consequences for the abuser or the victim. But with God's help, there's another step we can take.

Moving toward compassion

Some time ago I was surprised to come across a card Walter sent me for my high school graduation. When I'd received it, I hadn't noticed anything extraordinary about it and piled it with the rest of my cards. Reading it later, I saw that Walter had written me a note on the back. There, in his own handwriting, were the words, "With deep regret for past mistakes . . ."

After years of believing Walter would never admit what he had done, God surprised me. Walter seemed to be taking a step toward responsibility for his actions. I couldn't believe it! And I had almost missed seeing his message! Though I'm sure he'll never fully understand the horrible effects of his abuse, it was very satisfying to read his words.

Miraculously God has been helping me see Walter through His eyes of compassion instead of through clouded lenses of hatred and fear. He has even helped me come to the point that I'm praying for Walter and his restoration to God.

Now I can move on and try to help others.

[1]Rich Buhler, *Pain and Pretending,* pp. 198–199.

Guidelines when considering reconciliation

- Reconciliation can't be forced or rushed. The survivor must be sufficiently prepared (e.g., grieve losses, express feelings, heal memories, grant forgiveness). Pray for wisdom and help from God.

- Reconciliation may not be safe. If the abuser hasn't received help in overcoming this sin, trying to restore a trusting relationship may only put the survivor in jeopardy again.

- The abuser must take responsibility for his actions. When the abuser continues in the darkness of denial, it is impossible to reconcile (1 John 1:5, 7).

- Don't expect "instant trust." Trust must be earned. Give it time.

- Don't have unrealistic expectations. The success of reconciliation may depend on the kind of relationship the perpetrator and survivor had before the abuse took place. The closer the relationship (family member, close friend) and the deeper the betrayal, the more difficult the reconciliation may be.

- Pray for your abuser. Leave the ultimate outcome in God's hands. If reconciliation isn't possible, don't seek revenge. Pray for healing in the abuser's life and ask God to bring that person into a right relationship with Himself. If the abuser is not repentant, remember that God is the Ultimate Judge, and abusers will have to answer to Him for all the pain they have caused.

CHAPTER **12**

Wounded Healer

For you, O LORD, have delivered my soul from death,
my eyes from tears, my feet from stumbling,
that I may walk before the Lord in the land of the living. . . .
O LORD, truly I am your servant. . . .
You have freed me from my chains.

Psalm 116:8–9, 16

I've come a long way from the girl who wanted to end her life to one who desires to help others find theirs. My secrets are all out in the open. God has lifted my burden of shame and given me a deep inner peace about all I've experienced. I've learned that bringing our brokenness to our Healer allows us to step into the light, where He created us to live.

Brennan Manning writes, "If we conceal our wounds out of fear and shame, our inner darkness can neither be illuminated nor become light for others."[1]

God has graciously restored my faith, hope, and joy—precious gifts from Him. I find hope in even little things.

Jesus promised, "Blessed are you who weep now, for you will laugh" (Luke 6:21). And He has certainly kept that promise.

There may still be times of grief and adjustment ahead for that little girl who was hurt so long ago. I know I'll have to face new issues if and when God allows marriage and children of my own. But I've come to a point of resolution because I've taken the time to focus on my inner wounds and bring them to God for healing. He has turned those hurts into painless scars—keys He can use to unlock prison doors other victims are hiding behind.

I've stopped asking why I was abused or why God didn't stop it. It happened. It affected me. I've faced it, and now I'm moving on as I ask a different question: How is God going to use what I've learned?

The best credentials

At first I'd been impatient for the day those nasty reminders of the past would disappear completely. Then God began showing me the invaluable gift they could be. If I would let Him use them, I could, in effect, become a "wounded healer."

October 22, 1997 (age 21)

Jody [my roommate] came back from church tonight, and she said, "Christa, I never realized this before, but you and I have the gift of laughter and joy." It's true. We've had so many fun times together. I don't think a day goes by that laughter doesn't fill our room. I'm extremely grateful because I well remember a time when I had forgotten what it was like to even smile. How things have changed! Recently, with friends, someone even said I was the biggest "laugher" in the group. God has allowed me to feel joy again!

A wounded healer, according to theologian Donald Joy, is a person who identifies with others who are in the midst of their own painful journey that begins with fear and ends with joy.

Referring to John 20:19–29, he says:

When Jesus entered the room after the resurrection and found the disciples huddled in fear, Jesus showed them His wounds in His hands and side and [the disciples] were overjoyed. (vv. 19–20). His wounds were the visible proof that they could relax and stop being paralyzed by fear. God is calling those of us with wounds, saying, "Come, work on them, know them, own them, do your grief work because your wounds are going to be your best credentials for effective care of other people."

I took great comfort in realizing that Jesus, though perfect in every way, still had scars on His body after His resurrection. He uses those scars to convince us that He can empathize with our suffering: "Since he himself has passed through the test of suffering, he is able to help those who are meeting their test now" (Hebrews 2:18 NEB).

His scars are evidence of the agony He endured, the shame He overcame, and the victory He won. Those scars released the disciples from their prison of fear and overwhelmed them with joy. Then they could freely take part in Jesus' glorious victory and draw others to Him. And so can we.

Comfort isn't the goal

I came to see my wounds—not as an ugly reminder of the past—but as a gift of hope for those hiding in darkness, searching for the light. God was calling me to action. William Wordsworth once wrote, "A deep distress has humanized my soul." I had seen the pain sexual abuse causes in other people's lives. I had heard their cries with my own ears. I knew their pain, their desperation, their ache for someone to care. How could I not respond?

Jesus held out His nail-scarred hand and lifted me out of the pit. And now He was empowering me to reach back into the pit—baring my own scars as evidence that I understand—to begin lifting other wounded souls out of the darkness.

Jesus said, "What I tell you in the dark, speak in the daylight; what is whispered in your ear, proclaim from the roofs" (Matthew 10:27). Commenting on this passage, Oswald Chambers writes, "When you are in the dark, listen, and God will give you a very precious message for someone else once you are back in the light."[2]

September 7, 1997

Satan loves to get to me by making me doubt the validity of what I am doing and making me focus on my insecurities, weaknesses, and lack of experience. Yet every once in a while God gives me simple reminders of why I'm doing what I'm doing.

I sit watching two little girls playing in the grass outside. They take turns lying down and rolling down the hill, laughing all the while. I'm tempted to join them. Their enthusiasm at such simple pleasures is infectious. It's this innocence, this spontaneity, and this sense of wonder that I yearn to protect in all children, for once these gifts from God are snatched away, it's a long and difficult journey to find them again. Thank you, God, for the renewed passion to do what I can to make a difference.

With all God had been teaching me, it followed naturally that I would somehow help others.

"Everybody, back in the pool!"

Author Mike Yaconelli tells a story about the Sunday John Perkins preached a sermon about Jesus healing the paralyzed man at the Pool of Bethesda (see chapter 4).

The animated congregation nodded and said their amens louder and louder as Perkins described how the healed man "grabbed his bed, leaped for joy, and went running down the street, shouting and praising God." By the time Perkins finished telling the story, the whole church was on its feet, dancing and praising the Lord.

Suddenly Perkins hollered out, "What a tragedy!"

Everyone hushed.

Then Perkins whispered, "What a tragedy that when this man was healed he did what everyone else did when they were healed; he left the pool! What we need in the church today are people who, after they've been healed, go back to the pool and help others in!"[3]

God gives us the privilege of reaching out to those who grieve from abuse and other sadness. And we can offer them "beauty instead of ashes. . . . They will be called oaks of righteousness, a planting of the LORD for the display of his splendor" (Isaiah 61:3). The Lord can use our suffering and scars to create a chain reaction, making one another strong in Christ—oaks of righteousness firmly planted in our communities to make a difference for Him.

I know I still have much growing to do, but I'm thankful for the people and experiences God has used along my journey to help me heal, grow, and learn what compassion and service are all about.

The gift of listening

God has been teaching me how to listen to people's words—and their behavior. I began to realize that my sensitivity may actually be a gift as I take time to listen closely. Through my years of silent pain too many people liked to talk and give advice, but rarely did anyone listen.

So I asked God to help me become a good listener because I knew that there's no better way to show you care. In His perfect timing, He has offered me opportunities to show hurting people that they are worthy of care and respect.

In my senior year of high school, my guidance counselor—knowing even then that I wanted to help others—asked if I would talk with a girl named Jenny. This fifth-grade girl was dealing with the effects of sexual abuse. As I drove to Jenny's house one Saturday afternoon, I prayed for courage and the right words that would make a difference in this hurting child's life. Still nervous, I pulled into her driveway. What would I say? How would she and her parents respond to me?

When will I learn that anxiety is pointless since God is in charge?

Jenny and I hit it off immediately. She was quiet, yet intelligent, matured by the hurtful experiences of an evil adult world. We chatted casually as we got to know each other. She told me about school and what she liked to do. Then, as we walked around her neighborhood, she described her abuse (at the hands of a trusted neighbor) and the ways it had affected her.

I could relate to everything she told me. I listened as she talked about the pain and shame she felt deep inside. Her honesty was refreshing and her spirit, though despairing, showed resiliency. I believed she would make it.

I bought her some ice cream, and we went to a park and sat under a tree, eating and talking. There was so much I wanted to say to Jenny, yet she seemed to have an understanding far beyond her years. I told her that she did the right thing by telling and that the consuming shame would someday be a faint memory. I told her some of my story,

> **P**raise be to the God and Father of our Lord Jesus Christ, the Father of compassion and the God of all comfort, who comforts us in all our troubles, so that we can comfort those in any trouble with the comfort we ourselves have received from God. For just as the sufferings of Christ flow over into our lives, so also through Christ our comfort overflows.
>
> 2 CORINTHIANS 1:3–5

too, hoping it would encourage her to keep fighting.

We took one final walk before I had to leave. I listened. She told me her peers treated her badly. Her self-esteem was low, her trust gone. I wanted to take away her pain and instill a sense of hope. Yet all I could do was listen, and that was what she needed.

Before I left, her parents thanked me repeatedly. But I felt I should be thanking them. I came intending to help a hurting girl, and somehow she helped me in the process. It's amazing how that works.

Two ears and a loving heart

I don't remember much of what I said, and I'm sure Jenny doesn't either. What I do remember is two girls who shared a common bond, walking around the block for hours—one talking, the other listening. One opening her heart, the other offering understanding. One sharing despair, the other sharing hope. I will never forget her words, "Thanks for listening" and the gift she insisted on giving me—a small, purple, ceramic horse she had painted—a gift

Wounded Healer

from the heart. It's one of the most valued things I own. As I drove home, I felt tremendous joy.

Jenny reminded me of myself when I was her age. I wished I'd had someone to talk to back then—someone who would listen to me and tell me I was okay, that what I was feeling was normal, and that I was going to make it.

I learned two important lessons during that day with Jenny:

1. Helping others is what life is all about.
2. Showing compassion doesn't take much—just two ears, a loving heart, and maybe some ice cream!

Restoring dignity

God has also been teaching me that every human being is precious to Him. In my first year of college, students were encouraged to do volunteer work in the community. One of the options was tutoring at the women's correctional facility. My interest was piqued when I heard that the majority of inmates were victims of abuse, but I was scared at the thought of going into a prison.

When I submitted my top three choices for service assignments, I ranked the correctional facility number three, thinking that if God wanted me there He would put me there. Somehow I knew He would. God again wanted me to risk, knowing that growth doesn't happen unless we face our fears.

I'll never forget our first day at the prison. Two friends and I arrived, filled with apprehension as the guard led us through at least four locked gates. I was afraid I'd never get out of there again as we were led farther and farther from

199

the freedom of the outside world. Knowing that some of these inmates might be violent, I feared for my safety.

But once we got to know them in the classroom, the women surprised us with their friendliness and sense of humor. One woman, pointing to another, whose leg was in a cast, whispered, "Do you know what she's in for? Murder. She robbed a bank and killed one of the guards!" Our eyes got really big and we didn't know what to say. Then she started laughing and told us she was just kidding. But we were definitely relieved, and the joking around broke the ice.

About once a week my friends and I tutored these women in spelling, reading, and math. Though most were in their 20s and 30s, their skills were only at about an eighth-grade level. They really wanted to learn. It was exciting to see them work hard and show good progress.

God opened my eyes during my time tutoring these women:

- I had arrived afraid and left feeling more confident.

- I had arrived seeing them as criminals and left seeing them as precious human beings.

- I had arrived feeling somehow superior and left feeling a common bond between us. They were people no different from me. They deserved compassion and respect just like anyone else. In fact, they longed for it.

Sometimes I had opportunities to talk to them about God, and sometimes all I could do was listen. But often that was enough.

January 1995 (age 18)

Today I helped a twenty-three-year-old with math problems, and we got into a good conversation. She told me she hadn't been home since she was fourteen. She was adopted and lived in foster homes until age eight. There's not much contact between her and her family at all. She feels they're really disappointed in the way she's chosen to live her life. I asked her if she's going to change her ways once she gets out, and she said yes. She's been thinking lots about that. She asked if I grew up in a Christian family. I said I was thankful that I had because it has provided me with hope. And that it's the most important thing in my life. She said she "used to be a Christian." She sometimes reads her Bible now and she still believes in Jesus. I can't believe how open some of these women are. I guess, like this woman said, they need hope. It's really exciting when I have positive interactions with the women here!

I identified with these women who were trying to cling to whatever dignity and hope they had left. I, too, had fought that battle and had the scars to prove it. Our life stories were all filled with pain that ended in imprisonment—for them behind steel bars, for me behind "steel" silence. The God who loves me and hears my cries is the same God who loves each of them and wants them to call out to Him.

Career guidance

As I continued to look for ways to reach out with a message of hope, God gave me a passion for working with teenagers, especially troubled ones. I understood their insecurities, their pain, and their struggle to find their way in this difficult world. In reading a lot about runaways, I'd discovered this startling fact: A large majority of each year's more than one million runaways have suffered abuse.

The more I learned about these kids, the more certain I was that God wanted me to pursue working with them as a career. He confirmed His leading a year-and-a-half later through an opportunity to work with a crisis hotline and shelter for runaways and homeless youth. That summer I again found a common bond through mutual suffering— even if the details of our lives were worlds apart. I understood these kids, for I saw myself in them. I related to their fundamental needs, feelings, and heartaches. Though I never physically ran away from home, I thought about it several times. Instead, I ran away inside myself to escape.

At the beginning of the summer, I knew my eyes would be opened to many things, but little did I realize how much. It's one thing to hear about what kids are doing and dealing with, but it's quite another to see it face to face every day. Had it not been for my deep faith in God and my own testimony of how God transformed my life, it would have been easy for me to give up hope of making an impact on these kids' lives.

Cycles of abuse

The situations many of them are running from are often so tragic that they hope a better life awaits them on the streets. Unfortunately, most soon find freedom and safety elusive as the danger of street life becomes reality. There are plenty of people out there eager to entice these young people down the wide road to destruction, but those lighting the way to Truth's narrow road are few.

Too many runaways face a cycle of abuse—running to escape a horrible situation at home, revictimization on the streets, more shame, and the shattering of what little self-esteem they have left. They're easy prey for the street "outreach" workers—the pimps, pornographers, and drug dealers.

The U. S. Department of Health and Human Services reports that at least half of the runaway population are victims of some sort of commercial sexual exploitation. It's the only way they can survive. And many find it nearly impossible to break free from this sickening cycle of abuse.

I started the summer at the shelter a little naive but excited and passionate about making a difference in kids' lives. I ended the summer less naive but excited about the vision God was giving me for a very needed ministry—and even more passionate about making a difference.

The need for a Christian presence

I was overwhelmed by the extent of the runaway problem and deeply saddened by the small number of services available to help with this huge need. Yet I was even more disheartened to see that a majority of what is there for runaways and homeless youth doesn't acknowledge God as the Ultimate Healer of hurting souls. These programs can help kids to a point, but they're missing the spiritual aspects entirely. I wondered how we, as Christians, could reach out more to help thousands of young people find their way Home?

Each conversation I had with these teenagers confirmed even more the urgency of reaching these kids with the truth of God's love and mercy. Their stories were shocking and heartbreaking. The vast majority came to the shelter because of conflicts with parents—or a parent, since many lived in single-parent homes. An overwhelming percentage had been abused in some way, used chemicals, and/or attempted suicide. Most struggled with poor self-esteem and/or depression, some with pregnancy or sexual identity issues. Some came to the shelter because of bad choices they had made, but a huge number came because of things that had been done to them—many times by people who were supposed to protect them.

I learned a lot that summer about love and compassion. In suffering we are all the same, for pain is not partial. It is our reaction to pain that makes us different: some become hardened, passive, angry, or violent. Others grow and are strengthened. Compassion from God helped me transcend prejudices and discover that at the core we are all the same and have much to offer one another.

These young people often spoke of wanting to kill themselves, or of depression, or their battle with low self-esteem, and I immediately connected with their pain and desperate need for someone to care. Even when they directed their deep anger at me, I wanted to love and care for them. I wanted to offer light and hope.

THE WOUNDED HEALER'S CREDO

Is not this the kind of fasting I have chosen: to loose the chains of injustice and untie the cords of the yoke, to set the oppressed free and break every yoke? . . . Then your light will break forth like the dawn, and your healing will quickly appear; then your righteousness will go before you, and the glory of the LORD will be your rear guard. Then you will call, and the LORD will answer; you will cry for help, and he will say: Here am I. If you do away with the yoke of oppression, with the pointing finger and malicious talk, and if you spend yourselves in behalf of the hungry and satisfy the needs of the oppressed, then your light will rise in the darkness, and your night will become like the noonday.

ISAIAH 58:6–10

I listened, talked with them, and tried to encourage, but I know my light didn't always shine brightly. My patience sometimes wore thin. I struggled with how to get past their walls and reach them. And God helped me discover more fully what it means to be a wounded healer, a broken human being transformed by God's mercy, who then carries His light to a world in need.

205

My opportunity to say thank you

Shortly after I began working at the shelter, God brought back memories of that dark night, six years earlier, when someone became a light for me through a crisis hotline. Now it was my turn to take hotline calls at the shelter, and I didn't feel ready. I had listened in on several calls the other counselors took, but when the phone rang and everyone else was busy, I felt scared. I wondered if I could find the right words to say. Nervously, and with a quick prayer for help, I picked up the receiver.

For nearly forty-five minutes, I listened and talked with a twelve-year-old boy who was struggling so much with his relationship with his mom that he wanted to commit suicide. He said he couldn't talk to her, and he was filled with rage.

"So many times I've thought about killing myself," he said, "but I can't go through with it because I'm afraid of what will happen to me after I die." He brought up the subject of God and church, but he said he was confused about what to believe because his family didn't believe in God.

My heart ached for this boy because I knew I had the answers he was looking for. *What a perfect opportunity to share my faith and the truth of the gospel,* I thought. Jesus loves him and He could be this boy's strength and comfort. But I was working at a secular shelter. My superiors in the room with me always laughed off Christianity, God, and absolute truth. So I didn't know what they would deem appropriate.

Mostly I listened to him and let him talk through his hurt, anger, and confusion.

"I know it isn't easy, but try to stay calm and talk to your mom," I urged him. "And listen carefully to what she's saying." I even urged him to go to church and talk to a pastor about his questions. At the end of our conversation he thanked me, and I felt hopeful that I had done some good.

I felt great satisfaction as I recalled what one woman's concern and compassion had meant to me years earlier when I mustered the courage to call a crisis hotline. In a roundabout way, I thought, I was finally able to "thank" her by being a light of compassion and hope for someone else in the midst of a dark time in his life.

I'm grateful for any way God can use me. I'm only a common, cracked vessel who has seen depravity's depths and joy's heights and has been mended somewhere between the two extremes by God's grace. All I can do is be available to Him. After all He is the Light. I'm just a lantern.

Healed people drawing hurting people to the Healer—isn't that what this life is all about?

Knowing my limitations

After all I'd been learning about helping others, I also had to learn to recognize when I was in over my head.

One of the most difficult, eye-opening experiences I've ever had was watching my friend Deanna relive her painful past through flashbacks—terrifying experiences, reliving all or parts of the original trauma without the defenses to block the pain. My friend had been physically not sexually abused, but the repercussions are similar.

Flashbacks may come like a movie running through the victim's mind, or they may be snapshots: smells, sounds, feelings, or body sensations. Because of their painful intensity, these episodes may seem like a step backward in healing. But actually they help victims find freedom from the secret long hidden.

I had never experienced flashbacks, so I didn't know what was happening when Deanna started acting strangely. "I can't deal with the abuse anymore," she said in despair.

I tried to encourage her, but my words fell flat, and she sank further into her pain.

"Where is he?" she asked repeatedly, looking for someone who wasn't there. Then her whole body flinched as if someone were hitting her. "Please stop!" she begged. "I'm sorry. I'm sorry. I'm sorry."

I tried to calm her, but she winced every time I tried to touch her. Horrified, I didn't know what to do. My heart ached for her. I hadn't known how real flashbacks were. It was as if I were watching the abuse take place. The agony, helplessness, horror, and despair overwhelmed me.

There wasn't much I could do for Deanna other than stay by her side while she faced her monster. One victim told me about a time she experienced a flashback and other people in the room laughed at her. They didn't understand what was happening. They didn't understand the depth of the pain being relived. This kind of response can damage the victim even more, so it's important to be aware of what's happening and to be supportive. Negative reactions only cause more shame, and then these episodes lose their healing value, sending victims back into the safety of secrecy.

Anyone experiencing or witnessing abuse flashbacks needs to seek professional help. Victims need trained counselors to help them through these fragile moments, not someone who runs in fear from the unknown or belittles the experience.

Riches in secret places

The abuse will always be a part of my life, for it helped shape who I am. But it is not my whole life, nor is it my identity. I'm simply Christa—not Christa the sexual abuse survivor.

God has given me victory. Satan must acknowledge defeat. His plan—to lock me up for a lifetime in silence, passivity, guilt, shame, despair, fear, and hopelessness—failed. I no longer consider myself a survivor of abuse (by definition, one who continues to function and exist despite being victimized). Instead, I have won. I have overcome.

Someone has defined overcomers as those who come out of the battle with more than they had going in. God has given me life. I am no longer a victim, nor am I just surviving. I'm living fully, freely, and passionately as God intended.

He says, "I will give you treasures of darkness, riches stored in secret places, so that you may know that I am the LORD, the God of Israel, who summons you by name" (Isaiah 45:3). Years ago, at the bottom of that deep, dark pit, I never dreamed God could redeem my painful past and mold precious gifts out of that permeating darkness. Only He could perform such a miracle.

Am I glad the abuse happened? No. But I'm profoundly grateful for all the lessons He's teaching me and the compassion for others He has instilled in me through my suffering. These are my treasures of darkness given by God who, by His grace and mercy, used Satan's evil to help me "take hold of the life that is truly life" (1 Timothy 6:19).

God has built within me an enduring faith, grounded in Jesus Christ, who wants to be the absolute center of my life. He is my Rock, my Refuge, my Strength, my Hope, my Peace, my Joy, my Source of Life, and my Light. "Whom shall I fear? . . . of whom shall I be afraid?" (Psalm 27:1).

I know full well that I'm not finished yet. I have many more lessons to learn and much more growing to do in the future, discovering more fully who God's calling me to be. But I'm thankful for His promise that "he who began a good work in you will carry it on to completion until the day of Christ Jesus" (Philippians 1:6).

I will extol the LORD at all times; his praise will always be on my lips. My soul will boast in the LORD; let the afflicted hear and rejoice. Glorify the LORD with me; let us exalt his name together. I sought the LORD, and he answered me; he delivered me from all my fears. Those who look to him are radiant; their faces are never covered with shame.

Psalm 34:1–5

[1]Brennan Manning, *Abba's Child* (Colorado Springs: NavPress, 1994), p. 162.

[2]Oswald Chambers, *My Utmost for His Highest,* February 14.

[3]Mike Yaconelli, "Loving Kids Into the Kingdom," *The Covenant Companion,* March 1997, p. 25.

Afterword

The painful journey out of the pit faded to the background as God journeyed with me toward wholeness. Had I not documented my pain and healing progress in writing, I would not have been able to write this book because I've forgotten so much. Reading through my journals does not cause me more pain but rather an increased gratitude for all that God has done in my life. He has kept His promise in Isaiah 54:4: "You will forget the shame of your youth."

I think back to the first support group meeting I went to when I was fifteen, and I realize how fortunate I am that I told my secret, started counseling, and began the healing process at such a young age. Most of the women there were in their late twenties to fifties. We had to take turns introducing ourselves and saying what our summer highlight was. For some of these women this was asking a lot. They feared things. They didn't trust. I think tears were a blink away for most of us.

That night I wrote in my journal: "These women have probably known pain all their lives, so they haven't experienced life to the fullest. I wouldn't want to be in their shoes for a minute."

Most victims don't get help. Then they face problems as adults, not realizing they can't resolve these problems until they root out the cause—the violation that happened years earlier. As we progress through adulthood, new issues—including marriage and parenting—come up. With the help I was getting, I began to realize that healing was a gift I was giving not only myself but also my future husband and children.

This is my story, yet it is every victim's story. Though the details may be different, we all long for healing and wholeness.

- Keep hope alive. Just as God brought me out of the pit and taught me to trust again, He will do the same for you. Hope may seem like an empty word and trust may seem to be forever lost, but remember, our God is a God of miracles, and He's waiting for you to ask (see Luke 8:50).

- Trust in God for healing. Perry Draper writes, "An oyster produces a priceless pearl that once started out as an irritant, a wound that needed to be healed. God is in the business of making something out of nothing."

- Depend on God for life. Make a conscious effort to rid yourself of everything from your past that's blocking your relationship with your heavenly Father and keeping you from realizing your full potential. Jesus wants us to experience life to the fullest (John 10:10). Satan will try to sidetrack you by telling you lies, but never give in to fear or give up the fight for wholeness. God will help you wage war against the Enemy (2 Thessalonians 3:3).

- Don't be afraid to take risks and to begin to trust again. Hold fast to the Lord's promise: "Do not fear, for I am with you; do not be dismayed, for I am your God. I will strengthen you and help you; I will uphold you with my righteous right hand" (Isaiah 41:10).

- Our Almighty God is more powerful than the Master of Deception. Victory is yours if you will allow God to begin working His miracle in your life. Break the silence and keep speaking words of truth. You will one day break free from your prison so that you may experience the abundant life God promises each of us.

- Be patient. Bringing your wounds to God's healing light can be painful in itself. A person who walks out of a dark room into the sunlight outside finds the brightness shocking and shades his eyes. But with patience the eyes adjust to the light, the pain ends, and the vision clears. In the end, the light helps rather than hurts. Wholeness is being able to look at and embrace each part of ourselves—even the ones tarnished by abuse—and to feel good about who we are.

- Keep fighting. I well remember the day filled with despair when my mom encouraged me to fight back so I could release the hold Walter still had on me after many years. The choice between life and death was up to me. I made my choice and so must you. I became determined to complete the journey from victim to survivor to overcomer. I refused to allow Satan to destroy me. God, in His mercy, granted me enough hope to hang onto so I could make it out of the pit. And as I did, I found the Light. I learned to trust again. I can only hope that you will choose to do the same.

> *May the God of hope fill you*
> *with all joy and peace as you trust in him,*
> *so that you may overflow with hope*
> *by the power of the Holy Spirit.*
>
> *Romans 15:13*

Note to the Reader

The publisher invites you to share your response to the message of this book by writing Discovery House Publishers, Box 3566, Grand Rapids, MI 49501, USA. For information about other Discovery House books, music, or videos, contact us at the same address or call 1-800-653-8333. Find us on the Internet at http://www.dhp.org/ or send e-mail to books@dhp.org.